Dash Diet & Mediterranean Diet Lunch Recipes

Quick and Easy DASH and Mediterranean Diet Lunch Recipes for Health and Weight Loss

Patty Goldman - Maria Greenwood

Table of Contents

Dash Diet

Lunch Recipes

Patty Goldman

Intruduction

The DASH Diet was created by a branch of the US Department of Health and Human Services. DASH stands for Dietary Approaches to Stop Hypertension. The US Department of Agriculture considers the DASH diet not only an excellent option for anyone facing hypertension or high blood pressure, but also an optimum eating plan for people of all ages and levels of health. DASH is a user-friendly, well-balanced way of eating that offers a ton of great choices. The recipes in this book focus on fresh, whole ingredients so that the transition to DASH is easy and delicious. The DASH eating plan was originally developed to prevent hypertension (high blood pressure) through dietary recommendations of the National Heart, Lung, and Blood Institute, an institute of the National Institutes of Health. In fact, "DASH" stands for "Dietary Approaches to Stop Hypertension." These heart-healthy guidelines were designed to minimize the intake of processed sugars, salt, cholesterol, and saturated fats while increasing the intake of nutrient-rich foods with the aim of lowering blood pressure, decreasing weight, and reducing the incidence of chronic disease. The main nutrients DASH focuses on include minerals (such as calcium, magnesium, and potassium), antioxidants, lean protein, and fiber (both soluble and insoluble). When the intake of these key nutrients increases, the body is better equipped to function optimally and to burn calories rather than store them as fat.

Research confirms that DASH measurably reduces blood pressure and body weight, particularly when coupled with regular exercise.

Many frustrated and seasoned dieters will admit that dieting is extremely difficult and is often a failed undertaking.

Commercial diets are notorious for promising astonishing results in a short amount of time, without much effort or deprivation of unhealthy habits. Rightfully so, people are skeptical about diets, due in part to so many failed attempts. That's where DASH differs. DASH doesn't make promises. In fact, it's not even really a diet. The word "diet" has come to indicate making some big temporary change in eating in order to achieve some physical change, at which point the "diet" is over. DASH is actually the complete opposite: a long-term approach to eating as a commitment to health. It is an eating plan designed to promote and support healthy lifestyle changes, making weight loss a very nice by-product of the plan!

1. Insalata di Farro (Farro Salad)

Serves 6

Ingredients:

- 1/2 cup roasted chopped zucchini (see below)
- 2 cups Italian semi-pearled farro
- 8 ounces chopped fresh mozzarella cheese
- 1 (8-ounce) jar roasted red peppers, chopped
- 2 tablespoons finely chopped fresh parsley
- 2 tablespoons finely chopped fresh basil
- 1/8 teaspoon dried marjoram
- Juice of 1/2 lemon

- 2 tablespoons extra virgin olive oil
- 1/4 teaspoon sea salt
- 1/2 teaspoon cracked black pepper

Directions:

ROASTED ZUCCHINI

2 zucchini, cut lengthwise into 1/4-inch slices

4 tablespoons extra virgin olive oil

4 tablespoons balsamic vinegar

1/4 teaspoon cracked black pepper

1/2 teaspoon dried Italian herbs

To roast the zucchini, preheat the oven to 400°F. Coat a cookie sheet with olive oil spray, and arrange the sliced zucchini on it. Drizzle with olive oil and balsamic vinegar, and then sprinkle with pepper and dried herbs. Place on the middle rack of the oven, and cook until the zucchini starts to wrinkle and is soft to the touch, 8 to 10 minutes.

Meanwhile, bring a large pot of water to a boil, adding a drizzle of olive oil to prevent the farro from sticking. Add the farro to the boiling water and cook 20 to 30 minutes, or until al dente. Strain in a colander and pour the farro into a large bowl. Mix the roasted zucchini and all other ingredients into the cooked farro. Toss well, and serve immediately. Serving this dish warm will melt the mozzarella, but it can also be served chilled.

Nutrition Facts *(amount per serving)*

Calories 189

Total Fat 8 g

Saturated Fat 4 g

Polyunsaturated Fat 0.3 g

Monounsaturated Fat 2 g

Cholesterol 22 mg

Sodium 757 mg

Potassium 195 mg

Total Carbohydrate 24 g

Dietary Fiber 4 g

Sugars 0.5 g

Protein 13 g

Calcium 26% • Magnesium 5%

2.   Asian Quinoa Salad

Serves 6

Ingredients:

- 2 cups uncooked quinoa
- 4 cups low-sodium vegetable broth
- 1 cup cooked, shelled edamame
- 1/4 cup chopped green onion

- 1 1/2 teaspoons finely chopped fresh mint
- 1/2 cup chopped carrot
- 1/2 cup chopped red bell pepper
- 1/8 teaspoon chile pepper flakes
- 1/2 teaspoon grated orange zest
- 2 tablespoons finely chopped fresh Thai basil
- Juice of 1/2 orange
- 1 teaspoon sesame seeds
- 1 tablespoon sesame oil
- 1 tablespoon extra virgin olive oil
- 1/8 teaspoon cracked black pepper

Directions:

Rinse the quinoa (if not prerinsed). In a small covered pot, bring the quinoa and vegetable broth to a boil over high heat. Reduce the heat to low and simmer for 10 to 15 minutes or until most of the liquid has been absorbed. Cooked quinoa should be slightly al dente; it is ready when most of the grains have uncoiled and you can see the unwound germ. Let the quinoa sit in the covered pot for about 5 minutes. Fluff gently with a fork and transfer the cooked quinoa to a large bowl, then mix in the remaining ingredients. Cool to room temperature and serve. This dish can also be served chilled.

Nutrition Facts *(amount per serving)*

Calories 331

Total Fat 10 g

Saturated Fat 0.7 g

Polyunsaturated Fat 2 g

Monounsaturated Fat 3 g

Cholesterol 0 mg

Sodium 103 mg

Potassium 95 mg

Total Carbohydrate 50 g

Dietary Fiber 6 g

Sugars 7 g

Protein 11 g

Calcium 3% • Magnesium 2%

3.   Chicken Pasta Salad

Serves 6

Ingredients:

- 8 ounces whole wheat penne pasta
- 1 (6-ounce) boneless, skinless chicken breast
- 1 cup halved seedless red grapes
- 1/4 cup walnut pieces
- 1 tablespoon red wine vinegar
- 1/2 cup chopped celery
- 1/2 cup low-fat plain Greek yogurt
- 1/2 teaspoon cracked black pepper
- 1/8 teaspoon sea salt

Directions:

Boil a large pot of water, adding a drizzle of olive oil to prevent the pasta from sticking. Add the pasta to the boiling water, stirring once, and cook 8 to 10 minutes, or until al dente. Strain the pasta.

While the pasta is cooking, trim the fat off the chicken, if any, and cut it into small cubes. Fill a separate, medium pot with water, and bring it to a boil over high heat. Add the chicken cubes (water should cover them), and boil for 5 to 6 minutes.

Drain both the pasta and the chicken. In a large bowl, combine the pasta and the chicken with the remaining ingredients, and mix well. Refrigerate for 20 to 30 minutes before serving.

Nutrition Facts *(amount per serving)*

Calories 115

Total Fat 4 g

Saturated Fat 0.5 g

Polyunsaturated Fat 3 g

Monounsaturated Fat 0.6 g

Cholesterol 16 mg

Sodium 84 mg

Potassium 165 mg

Total Carbohydrate 11 g

Dietary Fiber 2 g

Sugars 3 g

Protein 10 g

Calcium 4% • Magnesium 7%

4. Healthy Italian Pasta Salad

Serves 4

Ingredients:

- 4 cups whole wheat penne pasta
- 1/4 cup toasted pine nuts

- 2 cups halved cherry tomatoes
- 1 cup chopped fresh mozzarella cheese
- 1 bunch coarsely chopped fresh basil
- 4 tablespoons extra virgin olive oil
- Pinch of sea salt

Directions:

1/8 teaspoon cracked black pepper

Boil a large pot of water, adding a drizzle of olive oil to prevent the pasta from sticking. Add the pasta to the boiling water, stirring once, and cook 8 to 10 minutes, or until al dente. Strain the pasta.

To toast the pine nuts, heat a large, flat pan over mediumhigh heat. Add the pine nuts, and stir frequently to avoid burning. Toast for about 2 minutes or until the nuts smell buttery and they are light brown on the outside. Remove them from the pan immediately.

In a large bowl, toss the cooked pasta with the remaining ingredients. The warm pasta will slightly melt the cheese.

Nutrition Facts *(amount per serving)*

Calories 388

Total Fat 15 g

Saturated Fat 5 g

Polyunsaturated Fat 3 g

Monounsaturated Fat 6 g

Cholesterol 22 mg

Sodium 254 mg

Potassium 72 mg

Total Carbohydrate 45 g

Dietary Fiber 5 g

Sugars 4 g

Protein 18 g

Calcium 27% • Magnesium 6%

5.   Balsamic Glaze

Makes 6 (2-tablespoon) servings

Ingredients:

- 2 cups balsamic vinegar

Directions:

In a large saucepan, heat the balsamic vinegar over low heat for 25 to 30 minutes. Just simmer it, and do not let it boil. To test, dip a wooden spoon into the glaze; if you run your finger over the back of the spoon, it should leave a clean line. Cool and store in a squeeze bottle to drizzle on salads, entrées, and desserts.

Nutrition Facts *(amount per serving)*
Calories 85
Total Fat 0 g
Saturated Fat 0 g
Polyunsaturated Fat 0 g
Monounsaturated Fat 0 g
Cholesterol 0 mg
Sodium 53 mg
Potassium 0 mg
Total Carbohydrate 21 g

Dietary Fiber 0 g

Sugars 0 g

Protein 0 g

Calcium 0% • Magnesium 0%

6.   Basic Vinaigrette

Makes 6 (2-tablespoon) servings

Ingredients*:*

- 1/2 teaspoon Dijon or brown mustard
- 1/2 teaspoon reduced-sugar marmalade (any fruit flavor)
- 1/4 cup balsamic vinegar (sweet) or red wine vinegar (acidic)
- 1/2 cup extra virgin olive oil
- 1/8 teaspoon sea salt

Directions:

Cracked black pepper
In a small bowl, whisk together the mustard, marmalade, and vinegar. Very slowly drizzle in the oil, and continue whisking the mixture together. (Constant whisking emulsifies the oil and vinegar, dispersing the droplets of one into the other and creating a thick dressing.) Add salt and pepper. Store in an airtight jar or container if not immediately using.
Note: It is recommend that the base for the homemade vinaigrette consists of 1 part vinegar or other acid, such as lemon, lime, or orange juice, and 2 parts oil.

Nutrition Facts *(amount per serving)*
Calories 170
Total Fat 19 g
Saturated Fat 3 g
Polyunsaturated Fat 3 g
Monounsaturated Fat 13 g
Cholesterol 0 mg
Sodium 62 mg
Potassium 1 mg
Total Carbohydrate 3 g
Dietary Fiber 0 g
Sugars 0.8 g
Protein 0g

7.Honey Lemon Vinaigrette

Makes 6 (2-tablespoon) servings

Ingredients:

- Juice of 3 lemons (about 1/4 cup)
- 1 tablespoon honey
- 1 teaspoon chopped fresh thyme
- 1/8 teaspoon sea salt
- 1/8 teaspoon cracked black pepper
- 1/2 cup extra virgin olive oil

Directions:

In a small bowl, whisk together the lemon juice, honey, thyme, salt, and pepper. Very slowly drizzle in the oil, and continue whisking the mixture together. Store in an airtight container or jar if not immediately using.

Nutrition Facts *(amount per serving)*

Calories 173

Total Fat 19 g

Saturated Fat 3 g

Polyunsaturated Fat 3 g

Monounsaturated Fat 13 g

Cholesterol 0 mg

Sodium 49 mg

Potassium 15 mg

Total Carbohydrate 4 g

Dietary Fiber 0.1 g

Sugars 3 g

Protein 0.1 g

Calcium 0.1% • Magnesium 0.2%

8. Lemon Vinaigrette

Makes 6 (2-tablespoon) servings

Ingredients:

- Juice of 3 lemons (about 1/4 cup)
- 1 tablespoon Dijon mustard
- 1 teaspoon chopped fresh parsley
- 1/8 teaspoon sea salt
- 1/8 teaspoon cracked black pepper
- 1/2 cup extra virgin olive oil

Directions:

In a small bowl, whisk together the lemon juice, mustard, parsley, salt, and pepper. Very slowly drizzle in the oil, and continue whisking the mixture together. Store in an airtight container or jar for future use.

Nutrition Facts *(amount per serving)*

Calories 102

Total Fat 10 g

Saturated Fat 1 g

Polyunsaturated Fat 3 g

Monounsaturated Fat 7 g

Cholesterol 0 mg

Sodium 79 mg

Potassium 81 mg

Total Carbohydrate 9 g

Dietary Fiber 3 g

Sugars 3 g

Protein 0.7 g

Calcium 3% • Magnesium 2%

9.   Garlicky Balsamic Vinaigrette

Makes 6 (2-tablespoon) servings

Ingredients:

- 1/2 teaspoon Dijon mustard
- 1 large clove garlic, finely minced
- 1/2 teaspoon reduced-sugar raspberry marmalade
- 1/4 cup balsamic vinegar
- 1/2 cup extra virgin olive oil
- Pinch of dried oregano
- 1/8 teaspoon sea salt

Directions:

Cracked black pepper

In a small bowl, whisk together the mustard, garlic, marmalade, and vinegar. Very slowly drizzle in the oil, and continue whisking the mixture together. Add the oregano and the salt and pepper.

Nutrition Facts *(amount per serving)*

Calories 66

Total Fat 7 g

Saturated Fat 1 g

Polyunsaturated Fat 1 g

Monounsaturated Fat 5 g

Cholesterol 0 mg

Sodium 90.1 mg

Potassium 3.7 mg

Total Carbohydrate 1.2 g

Dietary Fiber 0.1 g

Sugars 0 g

Protein 0 g

Calcium 0.2% • Magnesium 0.1%

10. Mexican Summer Salad

Serves 6

Ingredients:

- 3 heads romaine lettuce, chopped
- 5 Roma tomatoes, chopped
- 1 1/2 cups sliced unpeeled cucumber
- 1/4 cup very thinly sliced white onion
- 1/4 cup fresh lime juice
- 1/8 cup extra virgin olive oil
- Sea salt
- Cracked black pepper

Directions:

In a large bowl, combine the lettuce, tomato, cucumber, and onion. Pour the lime juice and oil over the salad, and toss well. Season to taste with salt and pepper.

Personal Note from Chef Anna: Growing up, my mother used to make this salad for my sisters and me as a side dish to many traditional Mexican dishes. It is simple, easy to make, nutritious, and versatile.

Nutrition Facts *(amount per serving)*

Calories 78

Total Fat 5 g

Saturated Fat 0.7 g

Polyunsaturated Fat 0.6 g

Monounsaturated Fat 3 g

Cholesterol 0 mg

Sodium 61 mg

Potassium 405 mg

Total Carbohydrate 9 g

Dietary Fiber 2 g

Sugars 0.2 g

Protein 2 g

Calcium 2% • Magnesium 5%

11. Grilled Romaine Salad with Garlicky Balsamic Vinaigrette

Serves 4

Ingredients:

- 2 tablespoons olive oil
- 1 head romaine lettuce (about 12 leaves)
- 1/4 cup feta cheese
- 1/2 cup halved cherry tomatoes
- 1/4 cup chopped walnuts
- Garlicky Balsamic Vinaigrette

Directions:

Separate the leaves from the romaine head, and wash and dry them. Heat a grill to medium-high, brush oil on both sides of each lettuce leaf, and place on the grill. Watch carefully and turn often, as the leaves can wilt quickly. Once char marks are visible, remove the leaves and place three leaves on four individual plates. Top the grilled lettuce with the cheese, tomatoes, and walnuts. Drizzle with 2 tablespoons balsamic vinaigrette, and serve.

Nutrition Facts *(amount per serving)*

Calories 152 (218)

Total Fat 14 g (21 g)

Saturated Fat 3 g (4 g)

Polyunsaturated Fat 4 g (5 g)

Monounsaturated Fat 6 g (11 g)

Cholesterol 8 mg (8 mg)

Sodium 109 mg (199 mg)

Potassium 126 mg (130 mg)

Total Carbohydrate 5 g (6 g)

Dietary Fiber 1 g (1 g)

Sugars 1 g (1 g)

Protein 3 g (3 g)

12. Healthy Cobb Salad with Basic Vinaigrette

Serves 4

Ingredients:

- 4 slices turkey bacon
- 5 cups spinach
- 1 cup sliced cremini mushrooms
- 1/2 cup shredded carrot
- 1/2 large cucumber, sliced

- 1/2 (15-ounce) can kidney beans, rinsed and drained
- 1 large avocado, pitted, peeled, and chopped
- 1/3 cup crumbled blue cheese

Directions:

Heat a medium-sized nonstick pan over medium heat, and coat with olive oil spray. Add the turkey bacon, cook until brown, and then flip and continue cooking, 5 to 6 minutes. Remove and rest on a cutting board. Crumble the cooled turkey bacon by hand, or coarsely chop.

Place the spinach on a large serving platter. Then arrange the mushroom, carrot, cucumber, kidney beans, avocado, blue cheese, and turkey bacon in neat rows atop the spinach. Serve with vinaigrette on the side.

Nutrition Facts *(amount per serving)*

Calories 232 (402)

Total Fat 14 g (33 g)

Saturated Fat 4 g (7 g)

Polyunsaturated Fat 1 g (4 g)

Monounsaturated Fat 5 g (18 g)

Cholesterol 23 mg (23 mg)

Sodium 612 mg (674 mg)

Potassium 797 mg (798 mg)

Total Carbohydrate 19 g (21 g)

Dietary Fiber 9 g (9 g)

Sugars 1 g (2 g)

Protein 11 g (11 g)

Calcium 13% (13%) • Magnesium 18% (18%)

13.   Asian-Style Lettuce Wraps with Peanut Sauce

Serves 4

Ingredients:

- 2 cups uncooked red quinoa
- 4 cups low-sodium vegetable broth
- 8 large butter lettuce leaves
- 1 cup chopped snow peas (in thirds)
- 1 cup bean sprouts
- 1/2 cup chopped red bell pepper
- 1/2 cup shredded carrot
- 4 teaspoons sesame seeds
- PEANUT SAUCE
- 1 cup and 6 tablespoons crunchy peanut butter
- 1 1/4 cup low-sodium vegetable broth
- Juice of 1/2 lime
- 1/2 teaspoon sesame oil
- 1/2 teaspoon low-sodium soy sauce
- 1/4 teaspoon ground ginger
- 1/4 teaspoon rice vinegar
- 1/4 teaspoon chile pepper flakes
- 2 tablespoons chopped green onion, white end discarded

Directions:

Rinse the quinoa (if not prerinsed). In a large covered pot, bring the quinoa and vegetable broth to a boil over high heat. Reduce the heat to low and simmer for 10 to 15 minutes or until the liquid has been mostly absorbed. Cooked quinoa should be slightly al dente; it is ready when most of the grains have uncoiled and you can see the unwound germ. Let the quinoa sit in the covered pot for about 5 minutes. Fluff gently with a fork.

Place 1/2 cup cooked quinoa on each lettuce leaf. In a medium bowl, combine the snow peas, bean sprouts, bell pepper, and carrots. In a small saucepan, combine all the ingredients for the peanut sauce. Bring to a simmer over low heat, and stir until the peanut butter dissolves. Pour the sauce into the bowl with the chopped vegetables. Toss well and spoon evenly on top of the quinoa in each lettuce leaf. Sprinkle sesame seeds on top of the veggies, and serve.

Nutrition Facts *(amount per serving)*

Calories 486

Total Fat 15 g

Saturated Fat 1 g

Polyunsaturated Fat 2 g

Monounsaturated Fat 2 g

14. Italian Veggie Pita Sandwich

Serves 1

Ingredients:

- 1 100% whole wheat pita (with pocket)
- 1 tablespoon prepared pesto
- 1/2 cup arugula
- 1 (1/4-inch-thick) slice fresh mozzarella cheese
- 1 (1/4-inch-thick) slice heirloom tomato

- 1/4 cup roasted red pepper (about 2 large pieces from jar)
- 1/8 teaspoon cracked black pepper
- **Directions:**

Warm the pita on both sides in a skillet over low heat. Remove from heat, cut the pita in half and split open, and spread pesto on the inside. Fill with arugula, cheese, tomato, and red pepper. Top with black pepper.

Nutrition Facts *(amount per serving)*

Calories 213

Total Fat 11 g

Saturated Fat 3 g

Polyunsaturated Fat 0.4 g

Monounsaturated Fat 0.1 g

Cholesterol 8 mg

Sodium 379 mg

Potassium 210 mg

Total Carbohydrate 23 g

Dietary Fiber 4 g

Sugars 2 g

Protein 6 g

Calcium 11% • Magnesium 8%

15.   Turkey Chili

Serves 8

Ingredients:

- 2 tablespoons extra virgin olive oil
- 1/2 pound lean ground turkey
- 1/2 cup chopped red onion
- 3 medium cloves garlic, minced
- 2 cups chopped fresh tomatoes
- 1 (15-ounce) can garbanzo beans, rinsed and drained
- 1 (15-ounce) can black beans, rinsed and drained
- 1 (15-ounce) can kidney beans, rinsed and drained

- 1 (15-ounce) can white kidney beans, rinsed and drained
- 2 1/2 cups chopped zucchini
- 1 tablespoon chili powder
- 1/4 teaspoon ground cumin
- 1/2 teaspoon dried parsley
- 1/2 teaspoon dried oregano
- 1/2 teaspoon dried basil
- 3 cups low-sodium chicken broth
- 1/8 teaspoon ground black pepper
- 1/8 teaspoon sea salt
- 1/2 cup shredded low-fat cheddar cheese, for garnish
- 1/4 cup chopped fresh cilantro, for garnish

Directions:

Heat the oil in a large sauté pan over medium to high heat. Add the ground turkey, onion, and garlic. Cook for 5 to 6 minutes, or until browned, stirring constantly and breaking up turkey chunks with a spatula.

Place the remaining ingredients in a 6-quart crock pot, and then add the cooked turkey mixture. Mix well, cover, and cook on high for 4 hours or on low for 8 hours. Check occasionally and add a little water if the chili becomes too dry. Serve in bowls, and top with cheese and cilantro.

If a crock pot is not available, cook in a large pot with lid on the stove over low heat. Check often and add broth if necessary, as the chili may get hotter and the liquid may evaporate faster on the stovetop than in a crock pot.

Nutrition Facts *(amount per serving)*

Calories 266

Total Fat 11 g

Saturated Fat 2 g

Polyunsaturated Fat 1 g

Monounsaturated Fat 4 g

Cholesterol 42 mg

Sodium 497 mg

Potassium 556 mg

Total Carbohydrate 24 g

Dietary Fiber 7 g

Sugars 3 g

Protein 19 g

Calcium 9% • Magnesium 8%

16. Vegetarian Chili

Serves 8

Ingredients:

- 3 tablespoons extra virgin olive oil
- 1/2 large red onion, chopped
- 3 large cloves garlic, minced
- 4 small zucchinis, chopped
- 1/2 cup chopped red bell pepper
- 1/2 cup chopped yellow bell pepper
- 2 (15-ounce) cans black beans, rinsed and drained
- 1 (15-ounce) can kidney beans, rinsed and drained
- 1 (15-ounce) can garbanzo beans, rinsed and drained
- 2 (15-ounce) cans low-sodium diced tomatoes
- 1 tablespoon chili powder
- 1/2 teaspoon ground cumin
- 1/2 teaspoon dried parsley
- 1/2 teaspoon dried oregano
- 1/2 teaspoon dried basil
- 1/8 teaspoon black pepper
- 1/8 teaspoon sea salt
- 3/4 cup low-sodium vegetable broth
- 8 tablespoons low-fat plain Greek yogurt
- 1 large avocado, pitted, peeled, and thinly sliced

- 4 tablespoons chopped fresh cilantro

Directions:

Heat the oil in a large pot over medium-high heat, and add the onion and garlic. After 3 to 4 minutes, add the zucchini and bell peppers. Sauté the veggies until the onion is translucent. Transfer to a 6-quart crock pot, and add the remaining ingredients. Cook on low for 4 to 6 hours, adding water if necessary. Serve in bowls, and top with yogurt, 2 slices avocado, and cilantro.

If a crock pot is not available, cook in a large pot with lid on the stove over low heat. Check often and add a little water if necessary, as the chili may get hotter and the liquid may evaporate faster on the stovetop than in a crock pot.

Nutrition Facts *(amount per serving)*

Calories 257

Total Fat 10 g

Saturated Fat 1 g

Polyunsaturated Fat 3 g

Monounsaturated Fat 6 g

Cholesterol 0.2 mg

Sodium 426 mg

Potassium 851 mg

Total Carbohydrate 35 g

Dietary Fiber 11 g

17. Kale Vegetable Soup

Serves 6

Ingredients:

- 2 tablespoons extra virgin olive oil
- 3 medium carrots, sliced
- 3 small sweet potatoes, diced
- 1 large yellow onion, chopped
- 3 large cloves garlic, minced
- 2 small yellow zucchini, cubed
- 1/2 teaspoon dried oregano

- 1/4 teaspoon chile pepper flakes
- 1/8 teaspoon sea salt
- 1 quart low-sodium vegetable broth
- 1 (14-ounce) can low-sodium diced tomatoes
- 1/2 teaspoon fresh thyme, chopped
- 2 cups coarsely chopped kale
- 1 (15-ounce) can cannellini beans, rinsed and drained

Directions:

Heat the oil in a large pot over medium heat. Add the carrots, sweet potatoes, onion, and garlic, and cook until they begin to soften, about 4 to 5 minutes. Add the zucchini, oregano, chile pepper flakes, and salt, and cook for 1 minute. Stir in the broth, canned tomatoes with juice, and thyme. Bring to a boil, reduce heat, cover, and simmer for an additional 10 minutes. Then add the kale and beans, and continue simmering until the kale is wilted and the sweet potatoes are soft, about 8 to 10 more minutes. Serve hot.

Nutrition Facts (*amount per serving*)

Calories 195

Total Fat 5 g

Saturated Fat 0.8 g

Polyunsaturated Fat 0.9 g

Monounsaturated Fat 3 g

18. Tuna Salad

Makes 4 (1-cup) servings

Ingredients:

- 1/4 cup chopped celery
- 1/2 jalapeño chile pepper, seeded and chopped
- 1/4 cup chopped Roma tomato
- 1/4 cup chopped red onion
- 2 (6-ounce) cans albacore tuna in water, no salt added, drained
- 1 teaspoon brown mustard
- 3 tablespoons low-fat plain Greek yogurt
- 1/8 teaspoon cracked black pepper
- 1 small avocado, thinly sliced
- In a medium bowl, combine the celery, chile pepper, tomato,
- and onion. Mix in the tuna, mustard, yogurt, and pepper until
- well combined. Top the salad with avocado slices, and serve.

SERVING SUGGESTIONS

• Try this salad atop a bed of spinach, and drizzle with red wine vinegar.

• Enjoy it as a dip with whole wheat crackers.

Nutrition Facts *(amount per serving)*

Calories 162

Total Fat 7 g

Saturated Fat 0.9 g

Polyunsaturated Fat 0.8 g

Monounsaturated Fat 4 g

Cholesterol 38 mg

Sodium 241 mg

Potassium 318 mg

Total Carbohydrate 32 g

Dietary Fiber 6 g

Sugars 1 g

Protein 21 g

Calcium 4% • Magnesium 5%

19.   Pomegranate Salad

Serves 4

Ingredients:

- 4 cups arugula
- 1 large avocado, pitted, peeled, and chopped
- 1/2 cup thinly sliced fennel

- 1/2 cup thinly sliced Anjou pears, thinly sliced
- 1/4 cup pomegranate seeds

Directions:

In a large bowl, combine all the ingredients, adding the pomegranate seeds last. Toss well, and serve with your favorite oil and vinegar dressing.

Nutrition Facts *(amount per serving)*

Calories 106

Total Fat 7 g

Saturated Fat 0.9 g

Polyunsaturated Fat 0.9 g

Monounsaturated Fat 4 g

Cholesterol 0 mg

Sodium 15 mg

Potassium 414 mg

Total Carbohydrate 12 g

Dietary Fiber 4 g

Sugars 4 g

Protein 2 g

Calcium 5% • Magnesium 7%

20. Beet and Heirloom Tomato Salad

Serves 4

Ingredients:

- 1 cup cooked, thinly sliced beets
- 6 cups mixed greens
- 1 cup green heirloom tomato, sliced and cut in fourths

- 1/4 cup toasted walnut pieces
- 1/4 cup crumbled goat cheese
- 1/4 cup balsamic vinegar
- Cracked black pepper, to taste

Directions:

Prepare the beets by cutting off the green stems and washing the beets. Cut off the very top and very bottom of the beet, and then peel off the thick skin. Place the beets in a small pot with about 1/2 to 1 cup of water, and steam over medium heat for about 15 minutes. Once cooked, let cool, and then slice and cut each slice into fourths as with the heirloom tomatoes.

Place the mixed greens in a large salad bowl, and top with the beets, tomato, walnuts, and goat cheese. Drizzle with balsamic vinegar, and grind cracked black pepper over the top.

Nutrition Facts (*amount per serving*)

Calories 168

Total Fat 10 g

Saturated Fat 3 g

Cholesterol 11 mg

Sodium 257 mg

Potassium 643 mg

Total Carbohydrate 156 g

Dietary Fiber 2 g

Sugars 6 g

21. Greek Salad with Lemon Vinaigrette

Serves 4

Ingredients:

- 4 cups chopped romaine leaves (about 2 large heads of lettuce)
- 1/2 cup halved cherry tomatoes
- 1/2 cup rinsed and drained, coarsely chopped canned artichoke
- hearts
- 1/4 cup low-fat feta cheese
- 1 teaspoon dried oregano
- 10 black pitted olives, rinsed, drained, and chopped
- 8 tablespoons Lemon Vinaigrette

Directions:

Combine all the ingredients in a large salad bowl, and toss well. Serve each dish with 2 tablespoons of the lemon vinaigrette on the side.

Nutrition Facts *(amount per serving)* *

Calories 69 (171)

Total Fat 4 g (13 g)

Saturated Fat 2 g (3 g)

Polyunsaturated Fat 1 g (4 g)

Monounsaturated Fat 0.3 g (3 g)

Cholesterol 2 g (8 g)

Sodium 311 mg (401 mg)

Potassium 255 mg (259 mg)

Total Carbohydrate 7 g (7 g)

Dietary Fiber 3 g (4 g)

Sugars 0.8 g (0.8 g)

Protein 3 g (3 g)

Calcium 10% (10%) • Magnesium 4% (4%)

numbers in parentheses are figures with vinaigrette

22. Caprese Salad with Balsamic Glaze

Serves 6

Ingredients*:*

- 5 large beefsteak tomatoes, cut into 1/2-inch slices
- 1 bunch fresh basil
- 1 pound fresh buffalo mozzarella cheese, cut into 1/4-inch
- slices
- 5 tablespoons Balsamic Glaze (page 89)
- 5 tablespoons extra virgin olive oil
- Pinch of sea salt
- 1/8 teaspoon cracked black pepper

Directions:

Arrange the sliced tomatoes on a large platter. Top each slice with a large basil leaf and a mozzarella slice. Drizzle balsamic glaze and oil over the platter, and then sprinkle with salt and pepper.

Nutrition Facts *(amount per serving)* *

Calories 334 (419)

Total Fat 24 g (24 g)

Saturated Fat 9 g (9 g)

Polyunsaturated Fat 2 g (2 g)

Monounsaturated Fat 12 g (12 g)

Cholesterol 43.8 mg (44 mg)

Sodium 408 mg (461 mg)

Potassium 70 mg (70 mg)

Total Carbohydrate 11 g (32 g)

Dietary Fiber 1 g (1 g)

Sugars 4 g (4 g)

Protein 19 g (19 g)

Calcium 51% (51%) • Magnesium 5% (5%)

numbers in parentheses are figures with glaze

23. Grilled Tomatillo Salsa

Makes 16 (4-tablespoon) servings

Ingredients:

- 20 tomatillos, husked and washed
- 1/2 small white onion, cut into large pieces
- 1 large whole jalapeño chile pepper, stem cut off
- 2 cloves garlic
- 3/4 cup fresh cilantro
- 1 cup water
- 1/2 teaspoon sea salt

Directions:

Heat a grill to medium-high heat. Place the whole tomatillos directly on the grill. Watch them carefully, rotating every 2 to 3 minutes and turning over to blacken on all sides. It's okay if they blacken or burn, as it will add to their flavor. They're done when they feel soft and squishy when picked up with tongs. Place cooked tomatillos in a pot and cover, so they continue steaming while the rest of the tomatillos finish grilling. Once all the tomatillos have been grilled, leave them in the covered pot for 15 to 20 minutes, until completely cooled. They will release liquid while they cool, which can be used in place of water or mixed with water, to make the salsa.

In a small pot over high heat, cook the onion, chile pepper, and garlic until they start to brown. After 2 minutes, add the tomatillo liquid or mix of liquid and water, and cover. Simmer for about 5 minutes, or until a fork easily inserts into the onion. Transfer the onion mixture, tomatillos (first removing any hard cores and leaving skin on), and cilantro in batches to a blender, and blend on low speed and then high until smooth. Salt each batch to taste. Store blended batches in an airtight container.

Nutrition Facts (*amount per serving*)

Calories 15.4

Total Fat 0.4 g

Saturated Fat 0.1 g

Polyunsaturated Fat 0.2 g

Monounsaturated Fat 0.1 g

Cholesterol 0 mg

Sodium 1 mg

Potassium 119 mg

Total Carbohydrate 3 g

Dietary Fiber 0.9 g

Sugars 2 g

Protein 0.5 g

Calcium 0.6% • Magnesium 2%

24. Red Mexican Salsa

Makes 12 (2-tablespoon) servings

Ingredients:

- 20 dried red chiles/chiles de arbol
- 1 large clove garlic
- 1/2 white onion, cut into large pieces
- 2 large Roma tomatoes, cut into large pieces
- 1/2 cup water
- 3/4 cup fresh cilantro
- 1/4 teaspoon sea salt

Directions:

Heat a large skillet over high heat. Add the chiles, garlic, onion, and tomatoes directly to the pan with no oil. Once the tomato skins and chiles start to blacken, remove the chiles from the skillet and place them in a small pot with the water. Cover, and simmer for 8 to 10 minutes to soften the chiles. Once the chiles are softened, transfer the cooked ingredients along with the cilantro to a blender. Blend on low speed, and cover the top with a kitchen towel so that steam can escape, but the salsa won't explode out the top of the blender. Season with salt to taste. Caution: This salsa is very spicy!

Nutrition Facts *(amount per serving)*

Calories 10

Total Fat 0.1 g

Saturated Fat 0 g

Polyunsaturated Fat 0 g

Monounsaturated Fat 0 g

Cholesterol 0 mg

Sodium 132 mg

Potassium 54 mg

Total Carbohydrate 2 g

Dietary Fiber 0.3 g

Sugars 0 g

Protein 0.2 g

Calcium 0.6% • Magnesium 0.7%

25. Grilled Chicken with Black Bean Salsa

Serves 4

Ingredients:

- 2 cups rinsed and drained canned black beans
- 1 large Granny Smith apple, chopped
- 1/2 small red onion, finely chopped
- 1 serrano chile pepper, seeded and finely chopped

- 2 tablespoons chopped fresh cilantro
- Juice of 1 large lime
- Juice of 1/2 orange
- 1/8 teaspoon sea salt
- 1/8 teaspoon cracked black pepper
- 4 boneless, skinless chicken breasts

Directions:

To make the salsa, combine all the ingredients (except the salt, pepper, and chicken) in a large bowl. Refrigerate for at least an hour to let the flavors meld.

Heat a grill or grill pan to medium-high heat. Season the chicken breasts with salt and pepper. Place them on the grill, and cook 4 to 6 minutes per side, or until the center of each is no longer pink. Divide the salsa on top of the breasts, and serve.

Nutrition Facts *(amount per serving)*

Calories 251

Total Fat 1 g

Saturated Fat 0.2 g

Sodium 232 mg

Potassium 431 mg

Total Carbohydrate 30 g

Dietary Fiber 9 g

Sugars 5 g

Protein 31 g

Calcium 4% • Magnesium 17%

26. Beef Tacos

Serves 4

Ingredients:

- 2 tablespoons extra virgin olive oil
- 1/2 cup chopped white onion, divided
- 1 cup chopped red bell pepper
- 1 large clove garlic, minced
- 1/2 pound 95%-lean ground beef
- 1/2 teaspoon dried oregano
- 1/4 teaspoon cracked black pepper
- 3/4 cup chopped Roma tomato
- 1 teaspoon chopped jalapeño chile pepper (seeded for less
- heat)
- 4 tablespoons chopped fresh cilantro
- Juice of 1/2 lime
- 8 (6-inch) corn tortillas
- 4 radishes, thinly sliced

Directions:

Heat the oil in a large pan over medium-high heat. Add 1/4
cup of the onion and the bell pepper and garlic, and cook for 30
seconds. Then add the ground beef, breaking up any large

chunks with a spatula. Cook for 5 to 6 minutes, or until the meat is no longer pink. Add the oregano and black pepper while the meat cooks.

In a separate bowl, combine the remaining 1/4 cup chopped onion, tomato, chile pepper, cilantro, and lime juice to make a salsa topping. Mix to incorporate evenly, and set aside.

Warm the tortillas in a flat pan over medium heat. Place two tortillas on four individual plates, scoop the beef mixture onto the tortillas, top with salsa and sliced radishes, fold, and serve.

Nutrition Facts *(amount per serving)*

Calories 294 Total Fat 13 g Saturated Fat 3 g Polyunsaturated Fat 2 g Monounsaturated Fat 5 g Cholesterol 33 mg

Sodium 73 mg Potassium 318 mg

27. Curried Chicken Salad Pita Sandwich

Serves 4

Ingredients:

- 2 (6-ounce) boneless, skinless chicken breasts
- 1/2 cup chopped carrot
- 1/3 cup chopped green onion
- 1/4 cup golden raisins
- 3/4 cup low-fat plain Greek yogurt
- 1 1/2 teaspoons red wine vinegar
- 1 teaspoon curry powder

- 1/4 teaspoon ground cinnamon
- 4 100% whole wheat pitas (with pockets)
- 2 romaine lettuce leaves, chopped
- 8 heirloom tomatoes, sliced
- 1/4 cup chopped toasted almonds

Directions:

Trim the fat off the chicken, and cut the breasts into fourths. Fill a medium pot with water, and bring to a boil. Add the chicken, and boil 8 to 10 minutes, or until the centers are no longer pink. Strain the chicken, and set it aside to cool. In a medium-sized bowl, combine the carrot, green onion, and raisins. Shred the cooled chicken with two forks, and add it to the bowl. Add the yogurt, vinegar, curry powder, and cinnamon, and mix well. Refrigerate for 30 minutes.

Warm the pitas in a large skillet over low heat, and then cut them in half and split open. Stuff each pita pocket with salad mix, top with almonds, and serve.

Nutrition Facts *(amount per serving)*

Calories 340

Total Fat 7 g

Saturated Fat 1 g

Polyunsaturated Fat 1 g

Monounsaturated Fat 3 g

Cholesterol 51 mg

Sodium 297 mg

Potassium 553 mg

Total Carbohydrate 41 g

Dietary Fiber 7 g

Sugars 3 g

Protein 32 g

Calcium 11% • Magnesium 14%

28. Chicken Fajita Wraps

Serves 4

Ingredients:

- 3 tablespoons extra virgin olive oil
- 2 (6-ounce) boneless, skinless chicken breasts
- 1 teaspoon dried oregano
- 1/8 teaspoon sea salt
- 1/8 teaspoon black pepper
- 1/2 large white onion, thinly sliced
- 1 large green bell pepper, thinly sliced
- 1 large red bell pepper, thinly sliced
- 4 100% whole wheat tortillas
- 1 cup rinsed and drained canned black beans
- 1 cup shredded romaine lettuce
- 4 tablespoons low-fat plain Greek yogurt

Directions:

Heat the oil in a large pan over medium heat. While the pan heats, remove the fat from the chicken breasts, slice them lengthwise about 1/4 inch thick and cut the longer pieces in half. Season with oregano, salt, and pepper. Add the chicken to the pan, and sauté until the pieces are no longer pink in the center, 5 to 6 minutes. Remove the chicken from the pan, and set aside. Add the onion and bell peppers to the same pan, and sauté until the onions are soft but not completely transparent, about 4 minutes. Warm the tortillas in a flat pan over low heat. Divide the black beans, lettuce, chicken, and sautéed peppers and onions among the four tortillas. Top with yogurt, wrap, and serve.

Nutrition Facts *(amount per serving)*

Calories 366

Total Fat 14 g

Saturated Fat 2 g

Polyunsaturated Fat 2 g

Monounsaturated Fat 8 g

Cholesterol 35 mg

Sodium 557 mg

Potassium 317 mg

Total Carbohydrate 40 g

Dietary Fiber 9 g

Sugars 3 g

Protein 24 g

Calcium 6% • Magnesium 10%

29.   Italian-Style Tuna Salad

Serves 4 (makes 4 cups)

Ingredients:

- 2 (5-ounce) cans albacore tuna in water, no salt added, drained
- 1/2 cup chopped Roma tomato
- 1/4 cup chopped red onion
- 4 tablespoons finely chopped fresh parsley
- Juice of 1 lemon
- 4 tablespoons extra virgin olive oil
- 1/8 teaspoon cracked black pepper

Directions:

Place all the ingredients in a large bowl, and stir to incorporate evenly. Let sit for 30 minutes before serving.

Nutrition Facts *(amount per serving)*

Calories 205

Total Fat 15 g

Saturated Fat 2 g

Polyunsaturated Fat 2 g

Monounsaturated Fat 10 g

Cholesterol 38 mg

Sodium 192 mg

Potassium 94 mg

Total Carbohydrate 4 g

Dietary Fiber 2 g

Sugars 0 g

Protein 19 g

Calcium 2% • Magnesium 2%

30. Chicken Alfredo with Whole-Wheat Bowtie Pasta

Servings: 6

Ingredients:

- 12 ounces whole wheat bowtie pasta
- 2 tablespoons olive oil
- 3 chicken breasts, boneless and skinless
- 2 cloves garlic
- 3/4 low-sodium chicken broth
- 1/2 cup half-and-half
- 3/4 cup grated Parmesan cheese
- 2 tablespoons fresh parsley, minced
- Freshly ground black pepper, to taste

Directions:

1. Cook pasta according to package directions. Drain and set aside.

2. In a large skillet, heat 2 tablespoons of olive oil over medium-high heat.

Add chicken breasts and cook until golden brown and done in the middle,

about 5-6 minutes per side. Remove from pan, slice into bite-size pieces, set aside.

3. Add remaining 2 tablespoons of olive oil to pan. Add garlic and sauté for

1 minute. Pour in broth and let it boil for about 2 minutes. Add half-andhalf

and whisk together. Continuing cooking, stirring frequently, for several minutes until liquid starts to thicken.

4. Remove pan from and add Parmesan cheese, chicken, and pasta. Season

with black pepper. Toss all ingredients together until well combined. If

sauce is too thick, add a little extra chicken broth to thin it down.

5. Serve topped with parsley and additional Parmesan cheese, if desired.

Nutritional Information (per serving)

Calories: 490

Sodium: 450 mg

Protein: 28 g

Carbs: 46 g

Fat: 19 g

31.   Simple Baked Chicken

Servings: 4

Ingredients:

- 3-4 pound chicken, cut into parts
- 2-3 tablespoons olive oil
- 1/2 teaspoon thyme
- 1/4 teaspoon sea salt
- Freshly ground black pepper
- 1/2 cup low-sodium chicken stock

Directions:

1. Preheat oven to 400 degrees F.

2. Trim off any excess fat from chicken pieces. Rinse and pat dry with paper

towels.

3. Rub olive oil over chicken pieces. Sprinkle with thyme, salt, and pepper.

4. Arrange chicken pieces in roasting pan.

5. Bake chicken in oven for 30 minutes. Lower heat to 350 degrees F and

bake for an addition 15-30 minutes, or until juice run clear.

6. Remove from oven. Let rest for 5 to 10 minutes before serving.

Nutritional Information (per serving)

Calories: 550

Sodium: 480 mg

Protein: 91 g

Carbs: 0 g

Fat: 19 g

32. Pasta Primavera with Shrimp and Spinach Fettuccine

Servings: 6

Ingredients:

- 1/2 pound fresh asparagus, trimmed, cut into 1-inch lengths
- 12 ounces spinach fettuccine (can substitute whole-wheat if desired)
- 2 teaspoons olive oil
- 3 garlic cloves, minced
- 1/4 teaspoon crushed red pepper
- 1 pound medium shrimp, peeled and deveined (thawed if frozen)
- 1 cup green peas, fresh or frozen
- 1/2 cup green onion, sliced thin
- 1 tablespoon lemon juice
- 1 tablespoon fresh parsley, chopped
- 1/3 cup Parmesan cheese, grated
- 1/2 teaspoon salt
- Freshly ground black pepper, to taste

Directions:

1. Fill a large pot with water and bring to a boil. Add asparagus and cook

until tender but still crisp, about 4 minutes. Remove from water with

slotted spoon and set aside. Add pasta to water and cooking according to

package directions. Set aside.

2. In a large skillet, heat olive oil over medium heat. Add garlic and crushed

red pepper and cook, stirring, for about a minute. Add shrimp, peas, and

green onion and cook, stirring, for 3-4 minutes.

3. Add reserved pasta and asparagus along with lemon juice, parsley, and

Parmesan cheese. Season with salt and pepper. Toss to coat.

4. Serve hot.

Nutritional Information (per serving)

Calories: 360

Sodium: 380 mg

Protein: 26 g

Carbs: 49 g

Fat: 6 g

33. Pork Tenderloin with Apples and Sweet

Potatoes

Servings: 4

Ingredients:

- 3/4 cup apple cider
- 1/4 cup apple cider vinegar
- 3 tablespoons maple syrup
- 1/2 teaspoon paprika
- 1 teaspoon fresh grated ginger (or 1/4 teaspoon dried)
- 1 teaspoon ground black pepper
- 2 teaspoons olive oil
- 1 12-ounce pork tenderloin
- 1 large sweet potato, peeled, cut into small cubes
- 1 large apple, peeled, cut into small cubes

Directions:

1. Preheat oven to 375 degrees F.

2. In a bowl, combine apple cider, vinegar, maple syrup, paprika, ginger, and
pepper.

3. In a Dutch oven or large ovenproof sauté pan, heat oil over medium heat.

Add pork tenderloin and cook, turning, until all sides are browned, about

8-10 minutes. Remove pan from heat.

4. Add sweet potatoes to pan around the pork. Pour apple cider mixture over

pork. Cover and bake in oven for 20 minutes or until tenderloin reaches

internal temperature of 145-150 degrees F.

5. Remove pan from oven and add apple pieces. Return to oven and cook,

uncovered, for another 8-10 minutes, or until tenderloin reaches 170

degrees.

6. Let sit for 10 minutes before slicing pork.

7. Serve pork with apples and sweet potatoes on side. Cover with any

remaining sauce.

Nutritional Information (per serving)

Calories: 280

Sodium: 240 mg

Protein: 20 g

Carbs: 40 g

Fat: 5 g

34. Steak Tacos

Servings: 6

Ingredients:

- 1 1/4 pounds sirloin steak, cut into strips
- 1/4 teaspoon salt
- Freshly ground black pepper, to taste
- 2 tablespoons plus 2 teaspoons olive oil
- 12 (6-inch) tortillas
- 1/2 red onion, diced
- 3 fresh jalapeno peppers, seeded and chopped
- 1/2 bunch fresh cilantro, chopped

- 3 limes, cut into wedges

Directions:

1. In a large skillet, heat 2 tablespoons olive oil over medium-high heat.

Add steak and sauté until browned on all sides and cooked through to

desired doneness, about 5-6 minutes. Season with salt and pepper. Remove

from pan to plate and cover to keep warm.

2. In same skillet, add 2 more teaspoons olive oil and allow to get hot. Add

tortillas, one at a time, and cook turning once, until tortilla is lightly

browned but still flexible.

3. To assemble tacos, place tortilla on a plate and top with steak, onion,

jalapeno peppers, and cilantro. Squeeze lime juice over top.

Nutritional Information (per serving)

Calories: 380

Sodium: 115 mg

Protein: 20 g

Carbs: 28 g

Fat: 21 g

35. Lemon-Orange Orange Roughy

Light and citrusy and cooks up very quickly.

Servings: 4

Ingredients:

- 1 tablespoon olive oil
- 4 (4 ounce) fillets of orange roughy
- Juice of 1 orange
- Juice of 1 lemon
- 1/2 teaspoon black pepper

Directions:

1. Heat oil in a large skillet over medium-high heat. Place fillet in skillet and

drizzle with orange and lemon juice. Sprinkle with black pepper.

2. Cover and cook for 5-6 minutes or until fish flakes easily with fork.

Note: Orange roughy can be substituted with any firm mild fish such as

flounder, sole, haddock, or tilapia.

Nutritional Information (per serving)

Calories: 140

Sodium: 140 mg

Protein: 19 g

Carbs: 8 g

Fat: 4 g

36. Orange Chicken and Broccoli Stir Fry

Servings: 4

Ingredients:

- 1 tablespoon olive oil or coconut oil
- 1 pound chicken breast, boneless and skinless, cut into strips
- 1/3 cup orange juice
- 2 tablespoons low-sodium soy sauce
- 2 teaspoons cornstarch
- 2 cups broccoli, cut into small pieces
- 1 cup snow peas

- 2 cups cabbage, shredded
- 2 cups brown rice, cooked
- 1 tablespoon sesame seeds (optional)

Directions:

1. In a bowl, combine orange juice, soy sauce, and corn starch. Set aside.

2. Heat oil in wok or large sauté pan. Add chicken and stir fry for 4-5
minutes or until chicken is golden brown on all sides.

3. Add broccoli, snow peas, cabbage, and sauce mixture. Continue to stir fry
until vegetables are tender but still crisp, about 7-8 minutes.

4. Serve over brown rice and sprinkle with sesame seeds.

Nutritional Information (per serving)

Calories: 340

Sodium: 240 mg

Protein: 28 g

Carbs: 35 g

Fat: 8 g

37. Mediterranean Lemon Chicken and Potatoes

Servings: 4

Ingredients:

- 1 1/2 pounds chicken breast, skinless and boneless, cut into 1-inch cubes
- 1 pound Yukon Gold potatoes, cut into cubes
- 1 medium onion, chopped
- 1 red or yellow pepper, chopped
- 1/2 cup low-sodium vinaigrette
- 1/4 cup lemon juice
- 1 teaspoon oregano
- 1/2 teaspoon garlic powder
- 1/2 cup chopped tomato
- Freshly ground black pepper, to taste

Directions:

1. Mix all ingredients except tomatoes together in large bowl.

2. Lay out 4 large squares of aluminum foil. Place equal amount of chicken

and potato mixture in the center of each square. Fold top and sides to

enclose mixture in packet.

3. Bake in preheated 400 degree F oven for 30 minutes or until chicken and

potatoes are cooked through. Packet may also be cooked on the grill.

4. Open packets and top with chopped tomatoes. Season with black pepper

to taste.

Nutritional Information (per serving)

Calories: 320

Sodium: 420 mg

Protein: 43 g

Carbs: 34 g

Fat: 4 g

38. Tandoori Chicken

Servings: 6

Ingredients:

- 1 cup nonfat yogurt, plain
- 1/2 cup lemon juice
- 5 garlic cloves, crushed
- 2 tablespoons paprika
- 1 teaspoon curry powder
- 1 teaspoon ground ginger
- 1 teaspoon red pepper flakes

- 6 chicken breasts, skinless and boneless, cut into 2-inch chunks
- 6 skewers (soaked in water if using wooden skewers)

Directions:

1. Preheat oven to 400 degrees F.

2. In a bowl, combine yogurt, lemon juice, garlic, and spices. Blend well.

3. Divide chicken evenly and thread onto skewers. Place skewers in shallow

baking or casserole dish. Pour half of yogurt mixture onto chicken. Cover

and refrigerate for 15-20 minutes.

4. Spray another baking dish with nonstick cooking spray. Place chicken

skewers in pan. Coat with remaining 1/2 of yogurt marinade.

5. Bake in oven for 15-20 minutes or until chicken is cooked through and

juices run clear. Alternatively, chicken can cooked on a grill.

Note: Serve over brown rice with steamed veggies on the side.

Nutritional Information (per serving)

Calories: 175

Sodium: 105 mg

Protein: 30 g

Carbs: 8 g

Fat: 2 g

39. Steak Smothered in Mushrooms

Servings: 4

Ingredients:

- 1 pound sirloin steak
- 1 tablespoon olive oil
- 1 1/2 cups mushrooms, sliced
- 2 tablespoons butter
- 1/2 tablespoon all-purpose flour
- Freshly ground black pepper, to taste
- 3 tablespoons balsamic vinegar

Directions:

1. Heat oil in large nonstick skillet over medium-high heat. Add steak and

cook, turning once, until desired doneness. Remove steak from pan and

slice into thin strips.

2. In same skillet, add mushrooms and butter. Sprinkle with flour and

continue cooking, stirring occasionally, until mushrooms start to brown.

About 5-6 minutes. Season with black pepper.

3. Add in vinegar and cook for an additional 2 minutes, stirring frequently.

4. Serve steak with mushroom mixture on top.

Nutritional Information (per serving)

Calories: 175

Sodium: 105 mg

Protein: 30 g

Carbs: 8 g

Fat: 2 g

40. Slow-Cooker Beef Stew Provencal

Servings: 10

Ingredients:

Bouquet garni

- Cheesecloth
- 1 bay leaf

- 1 stalk celery, chopped
- 3 sprigs fresh parsley
- 3 sprigs fresh thyme
- *Stew*
- 2 tablespoons extra-virgin olive oil, divided
- 3 pounds beef chuck (or other stew meat), cut into 1-inch pieces
- 2 teaspoons kosher salt, divided
- 1/2 teaspoon freshly ground pepper, divided
- 2 medium yellow onions, chopped
- 4 cloves garlic, minced
- 3-4 large carrots, sliced into 1-inch rounds
- 2 tablespoons tomato paste, no salt added
- 1 pound mushrooms, sliced
- 1 quart beef stock, low-sodium
- 1/4 cup red wine

Directions:

1. To assemble bouquet garni, cut a square of cheesecloth. Place bay leaf,

celery, parsley, and thyme in center. Tie with kitchen twine.

2. To prepare stew heat 1 tablespoon olive oil in large heavy-duty pan. Add

beef cubes and until browned on all sides. Transfer to slow cooker, season

with 1 teaspoon salt and black pepper.

3. Add another tablespoon of oil to pan and add onions, garlic, and carrots.

Cook, stirring occasionally until they begin to soften, about 4-5 minutes.

Season with remaining salt and pepper. Add to slow cooker with beef.

4. Add tomato paste, mushrooms, beef stock, red wine, and bouquet garni to

slow cooker. Stir to combine.

5. Cover and cook on low setting for 8-9 hours or high setting for 5-6 hours.

Nutritional Information (per serving)

Calories: 351

Sodium: 380 mg

Protein: 26 g

Carbs: 14 g

Fat: 15 g

41.   Panko-Crusted Cod

Servings: 2

Ingredients:

- 1/4 Panko-style breadcrumbs
- 1 clove garlic, minced
- 1 tablespoon extra-virgin olive oil
- 3 tablespoons nonfat Greek yogurt
- 1 tablespoon mayonnaise
- 1 1/2 teaspoons lemon juice
- 1/2 teaspoon tarragon
- Pinch of salt
- 10 ounces cod, cut into two portions

Directions:

1. Preheat oven to 425 degrees F. Coat baking pan with nonstick cooking

spray.

2. In a small bowl, combine breadcrumbs, garlic and olive oil.

3. In another bowl, combine yogurt, mayonnaise, lemon juice, tarragon, and

salt.

4. Place fish in baking pan. Top each piece with one half yogurt mixture and

then 1/3 breadcrumb mixture.

5. Bake in oven for 15 minutes or until fish is opaque in center and

breadcrumbs are golden brown.

Nutritional Information (per serving)

Calories: 225

Sodium: 270 mg

Protein: 18 g

Carbs: 13 g

Fat: 10 g

42. Grilled Salmon and Asparagus with Lemon Butter

Servings: 4

Ingredients:

- 1 1/4 pounds salmon, cut into 4 portions
- 2 bunches asparagus, ends trimmed
- Cooking spray, preferably olive oil
- 1/2 teaspoon salt
- 1/4 teaspoon freshly ground pepper
- 1/4 teaspoon garlic powder
- 1 tablespoon olive oil
- 1 tablespoon butter
- 3 tablespoons lemon juice

Directions:

1. Place salmon and asparagus on large rimmed baking sheet. Spray lightly
with cooking spray. Sprinkle with salt, pepper, and garlic powder.

2. Place asparagus and salmon on preheated, oiled grill. Grill the salmon,
turning once, until opaque, about 3-5 minutes per side. Grill the asparagus,

turning occasionally, until tender, about 5-7 minutes.

3. In a microwave-safe bowl, place olive oil, butter, and lemon juice.

Microwave to melt butter, about 20 seconds. Drizzle fish with butterlemon

mixture. Serve immediately.

Note: This can also be cooked under the broiler instead of the grill.

Nutritional Information (per serving)

Calories: 190

Sodium: 445 mg

Protein: 24 g

Carbs: 6 g

Fat: 8 g

43. Slow-Cooker Turkey Stroganoff

Servings: 6

Ingredients:

- 4 cups mushrooms, sliced (can use a mix of types)
- 3 medium carrots, sliced into 1-inch rounds
- 1 small onion, chopped fine
- One 3-4 pound split turkey breast, skin removed (can substitute with
- chicken breast)
- 1/3 cup all-purpose flour
- 1 cup nonfat Greek-style plain yogurt

- 1 tablespoon lemon juice
- 1/4 dry sherry (not cooking sherry)
- 1 cup frozen peas, thawed
- Freshly ground black pepper, to taste
- 12 ounces whole-wheat egg noodles, cooked
- 1/4 cup flat-leaf parsley, chopped

Directions:

1. Place mushrooms, carrots, onion, and turkey in a 5-6 quart slow cooker.
Cover and cook on low for 8 hours or on high for 4 hours.

2. Remove turkey and place on cutting board.

3. In a bowl, whisk together flour, yogurt, lemon juice, and sherry. Add to
slow cooker along with peas and pepper. Stir, cover, and cook on high for
about 15 minutes.

4. Remove turkey meat from bone and cut into bite-size pieces. Place turkey
pieces back in slow cooker and stir.

5. Serve over egg noodles and top with chopped parsley.

Nutritional Information (per serving)

Calories: 440

Sodium: 480 mg

Protein: 46 g

Carbs: 43 g

Fat: 6 g

44. Oven-Barbecued Pork Chops

Servings: 4

Ingredients:

- 4 bone-in 3/4-inch thick pork chops (about 1 1/2 pounds)
- 1/4 teaspoon salt
- 1/4 teaspoon freshly ground black pepper
- 1 tablespoon plus 1 teaspoon olive oil
- 1 medium onion , diced
- 3 cloves garlic, minced
- 1/3 cup orange juice
- 1/2 cup low-sodium barbecue sauce

Directions

1. Preheat oven to 400 degrees F.

2. Heat 1 tablespoon olive oil in ovenproof skillet over high heat. Add pork

chops, season with salt and pepper, and cook until browned, 1 to 2 minutes

per side. Transfer to plate.

3. Add remaining 1 teaspoon olive oil to pan. Add onion and garlic and

cook, stirring, until softened, 3-4 minutes. Add orange juice and continue cooking until most of liquid is evaporated, 2-3 minutes. Add in barbecue

sauce, stir.

4. Return pork chops to pan, turning to coat with sauce.

5. Transfer pan to oven and bake until pork chops are cooked (internal

temperature of 145 F), about 7-8 minutes.

6. Serve pork chops topped with sauce.

Nutritional Information (per serving)

Calories: 245

Sodium: 390 mg

Protein: 20 g

Carbs: 15 g

Fat: 10 g

45. Whole-Wheat Spaghetti with Ragu Sauce

Servings: 8

Ingredients:

- 1 box whole-wheat spaghetti
- 1 tablespoon extra-virgin olive oil
- 1 medium onion, chopped fine
- 1 large carrot, chopped fine
- 1 stalk celery, chopped fine
- 4 cloves garlic, minced
- 1 teaspoon oregano
- 1 teaspoon basil
- 1 teaspoon marjoram
- 1 pound lean ground beef
- 1 28-ounce can crushed tomatoes, no salt added
- 1/2 teaspoon salt
- 1/4 cup flat-leaf parsley, chopped
- 1/2 cup grated Parmesan cheese

Directions:

1. Cook spaghetti according to package directions. Drain.

2. While pasta cooks, heat oil in large skillet over medium heat. Add onion,

carrot, and celery and cooking, stirring occasionally, until onion turns

translucent, about 5 minutes. Add in garlic and seasonings, and cook for

another 30 seconds.

3. Add beef and cook, stirring, until meat is browned and no longer pink,

about 4-5 minutes. Add crushed tomatoes and continue to cook, stirring

occasionally, until sauce thickens, about 5 minutes. Season with salt and

add parsley.

4. To serve, plate 1 cup of pasta, top with sauce and sprinkle with Parmesan

cheese.

Note: Sauce can be made ahead and kept in the refrigerator for up to 3 days.

Nutritional Information (per serving)

Calories: 385

Sodium: 415 mg

Protein: 28 g

Carbs: 52 g

Fat: 9 g

46. Sausage and Chicken Stew

Servings: 8

Ingredients:

- 1 tablespoon extra-virgin olive oil
- 8 ounces chorizo sausage, diced
- 2 medium yellow onions, chopped
- 3 cloves garlic, minced
- 3 pounds chicken thighs, boneless and skinless, cut into 1-inch pieces
- 2 tablespoons paprika
- 1/2 teaspoon sea salt
- Freshly ground black pepper, to taste
- 3 cups white wine

- 2 14.5 ounce cans diced tomatoes, no salt added
- 2 cups low-sodium chicken broth
- 1/4 cup flat-leaf parsley, chopped
- 1 pinch saffron

Directions:

1. In a large pot or Dutch oven, heat oil over medium heat. Add sausage and
cook, stirring occasionally, for 6-7 minutes. Add onion and garlic, and
continue to cook, stirring occasionally for 8-10 minutes, until onion is soft.

2. Add chicken, paprika, salt, and pepper, stir to coat. Cook for another 5
minutes, stirring occasionally.

3. Add wine, turn heat to high and cook until wine is reduced by a third,
about 7-8 minutes.

4. Add tomatoes, chicken broth, parsley, and saffron. Reduce heat to low
and simmer, uncovered, until sauce has thickened and chicken is tender,
about 1 hour.

5. Season with additional pepper, to taste.

Nutritional Information (per serving)

Calories: 185

Sodium: 230 mg

Protein: 16 g

Carbs: 7 g

47.   Quick and Easy Chili

Servings: 6

Ingredients:

- 1/2-pound lean ground beef
- 1/2 medium yellow onion, diced
- 1 can (15.5) low-sodium kidney beans, drained
- 1 can (14.5 ounces) diced tomatoes
- 1 1/2 tablespoons chili powder

Directions:

1. In a large skillet brown ground meat and onions over medium-high heat

(about 6-7 minutes). Drain excess fat.

2. Add beans, tomatoes, and chili powder.

3. Reduce heat to low, cover, and simmer for 10 minutes.

4. Serve with brown rice.

Nutritional Information (per serving)

Calories: 220

Sodium: 430 mg

Protein: 16 g

Carbs: 21 g

Fat: 7 g

Mediterranean Diet Lunch Recipes

Maria Greenwood

Introduction

The Basics of the Mediterranean Diet

The foods that we eat have been known to contribute greatly to how our health turns out. Feeding on unhealthy foods is known to cause a myriad of health issues, including chronic diseases; therefore, the diet that one adopts should be given a lot of emphasis. The Mediterranean diet is considered as one of the world's healthiest diet. It's an eating approach that puts emphasis on eating whole foods that are full of flavor. It's a diet that is abundant in fruits, whole grains, vegetables, legumes and olive oil. The diet also features lean sources of protein, and the red wine is consumed in moderate amounts.

The Mediterranean diet is also one of the top most popular diets, and it's not the type of diet where the end goal is only to lose weight; it's considered more of a lifestyle. It should be adopted as a daily practice and a way of living that's sustainable. The Mediterranean diet incorporates traditional and healthy living habits of people from the countries that border the Mediterranean Sea, such as Greece, Italy, France, Spain, Morocco and the like.

The diet varies by country and the region it is adopted, so it may have a range of definitions. However, it is a diet with high intake of vegetables, legumes, fruits, nuts, beans, grains, unsaturated fats like olive oil and fish among others. It, however, includes lower intake of dairy foods and meat. There are several benefits that have been associated with the Mediterranean diet, such as good health and a healthier heart.

Various research studies have proven that those who put a lot of emphasis on healthy fats, whole grains and fish not only weigh less but also experience decreased risks of heart-related diseases, dementia and depression.

Eating in this way means that one gets little room for consuming the unhealthy junk and processed foods, which normally lead to being overweight and obese

48.   Lentil Cream Soup

Total Time: 80 minutes

Ingredients:

- 9 oz red lentil
- 1 onion

- 2 tomatoes
- 1 carrot
- 2 garlic cloves
- 2 slices whole-grain bread
- 1 tsp ginger powder

Instructions:

1.Wash lentil in cold water and boil until done. The cooking time is 60 minutes.

2.Peel the onion. Chop tomatoes and onion into large cubes.

3.Peel and grate carrot, crush garlic.

4.Add all ingredients to boiled lentil in a saucepan and simmer for 15 minutes.

Beat with blender to uniformity.

5.Chop bread into cubes, dry on a dry frying pan. When serving, decorate with

bread croutons.

Nutrients per one serving:

Calories: 264 | Fats: 19 g | Carbs: 4.8 g | Proteins: 8 g

49.   Pashian Tuna Salad

Total Time: 15 minutes

Ingredients:

2 tbsp plain Greek yogurt

¼   cup cottage cheese 2 tsp Italian dressing

2 medium tomatoes, cut into wedges

2 cans 3 oz white tuna in water, flaked and drained 8 stuffed green olives, sliced

Instructions:

1.   In a small bowl, combine cottage cheese, dressing and mayo. Lightly mix in tuna and olives.
2.   Place in a serving plate with tomato wedges and serve as desired.

Nutrients per one serving:

270 Calories, 17g total fat 3g sat , 35mg cholesterol, 760mg sodium, 7g carbohydrate, 2g dietary fiber, 5g sugars, 20g protein.

50.   Feta Shrimp Skillet

Total Time: 30 minutes

Ingredients:

- Olive oil – 1 tablespoon
- Finely chopped medium onion – 1
- Minced garlic cloves - 3
- Pepper – ½ teaspoon
- Diced tomatoes – 2 cans
- Uncooked shrimp peeled and deveined – 1 pound
- Minced fresh parsley – 2 tablespoons
- Crumbled feta cheese – ¾ cup

- Dried oregano – 1 teaspoon
- Salt and pepper to taste
- White wine – ¼ cup optional

Instructions

1.   Place a large non-stick skillet over medium heat and then add oil and heat. Add onion. Cook for about 4 minutes as you occasionally stir.

2.   Add seasonings and garlic and then cook for one more minute. Stir in tomatoes as desired and wine. After which, bring to a boil.

3.   Reduce heat and then allow to simmer for 7 minutes uncovered or until the sauce is thickened.

4.   Add shrimp and parsley and cook for 6 minutes or until shrimp turns pink as you occasionally stir.

5.   Remove from heat once cooked and then sprinkle with cheese and allow to stay covered for some time until the cheese softens.

6.   Serve and enjoy.

Nutrients per one serving:

Calories per serving: 240; Carbohydrates: 9g; Protein: 25g; Fat: 11g; Sugar: 4g; Sodium: 748mg; Fiber: 5g

51. **Veggie Cream Soup**

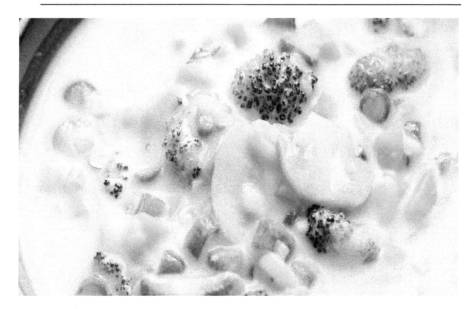

Total Time: 20 minutes

Ingredients:

- 1 leek
- 1 onion
- 3 potatoes
- 1 bell pepper
- 1 cauliflower head
- 3 tbsp butter
- A pinch of salt and Provence herbs

Instructions:

1.Pre-cook veggies: peel and chop onions into half rings. Cut pepper and remove the middle, chop into slices. Crush leek. Peel and cut potatoes into

small cubes. Cut cauliflower into small inflorescences.

2.Heat the frying pan, add butter and fry the onion.

3.Add other vegetables into onion fry them and lay out in a pan for cooking.

Add the necessary amount of water and put on a plate. Boil vegetables for 12 minutes.

4.Beat with blender, season with salt and pepper.

Nutrients per one serving:

Calories: 247 | Fats: 16 g | Carbs: 5 g | Proteins: 10 g

52.   Panzanella

Total Time: 15 minutes

Ingredients:
- 7 cherry tomatoes
- 1 bell pepper
- 1 red onion
- 5 bread slices
- 2 tbsp olive oil
- 1 tbsp wine vinegar
- A pinch of ground black pepper
- A pinch of Italian dry herbs

- A bunch of fresh basil

Instructions:

1.Wash up veggies. Chop the tomatoes into halves, peel the bell pepper and
chop into strips.

2.Peel and chop the onion into slices.

3.Dice bread and slightly dried in an oven or pan.

4.Put bread, tomatoes, onions, and peppers in a salad bowl. Add the basil.

5.In a separate bowl, mix the olive oil, spices, and vinegar.

6.Pour the dressing into salad and mix well. Cool for 5 minutes in the refrigerator.

Nutrients per one serving:

Calories: 128 | Fats: 16 g | Carbs: 4.8 g | Proteins: 9 g

53. Sian Chicken Salad

Total Time: 10 minutes

Ingredients:

- 1 cup roasted chicken breast,
- 2 tbsp green onions
- 2 tbsp pine nuts, toasted
- ½ cup chopped celery 1 tbsp chopped basil
- Dressing:
- 2 tbsp plain Greek yogurt
- ½ tbsp lemon juice 1 tbsp sour cream Lettuce leaves
- Pinch of salt and chili flakes

Instructions:

1. In a bowl, mix all the salad ingredients.

2. In another small bowl, mix Ingredients for the dressing. Combine with the salad mixture. Toss well. Serve in a bed of lettuce leaves.

54. Healthy Tuscan Chicken

Total Time: 40 min| Serves 4

Ingredients

- Boneless skinless chicken breast – 4 6 ounces
- Pepper – ¼ teaspoon
- Green, red and yellow peppers julienned – 1

- Chicken broth – 1 can
- Minced fresh basil – 2 tablespoons
- Dried basil – 2 teaspoons
- Minced fresh oregano – 1 teaspoon
- Olive oil – 2 tablespoons
- Minced garlic cloves – 2

Instructions

1.   Sprinkle the chicken with salt and pepper and then set aside. Place a skillet over medium heat and then add oil and heat.

2.   Add chicken and then cook until brown. After which, remove from heat and set aside. In the same skillet, add chopped deli ham and peppers. Cook until the peppers are tender.

3.   Add garlic into the pan and then cook for a minute. Add tomatoes, basil, broth, oregano and chicken and then bring to a boil. Reduce heat and then cover and allow to simmer for 15 minutes or until the thermometer reads 1700.

4.   Serve and enjoy.

Nutrients per one serving:

Calories: 304; Carbohydrates: 11g; Protein: 38g; Fat: 12g; Sugar: 4g; Sodium:389mg; Fiber: 3g

55. Feta Salad

Total Time: 15 minutes

Ingredients:

- 7.5 oz feta
- 7 tomatoes
- 3 oz pomegranate grains
- A bunch of fresh cilantro
- A pinch of ground pepper
- 1 tsp balsamic vinegar
- A pinch of salt

Instructions:

1.Wash and chop tomatoes into thin circles. Chop the feta into thin slices and
fry on a dry frying pan for 1 minute.

2.Put feta, tomatoes, pomegranate grains, finely chopped cilantro in a salad
bowl. Mix well. Season with vinegar, salt, and pepper.

Nutrients per one serving:

Calories: 165 | Fats: 13 g | Carbs: 8 g | Proteins: 19 g

56.   Whole Orzo Salad

Total Time: 1 hour and 20 minutes

Ingredients:

- 2 cups whole wheat orzo, cooked per Instructions 1/3 cup Kalamata olives, pitted and halved

- ¼ cup diced sundried tomatoes 1 ½ tbsp olive oil
- ½ cup cubed feta
- ¼ cup pine nuts, toasted
- 1 tbsp lemon juice
- 1 tbsp diced fresh parsley
- Salt and pepper to taste

Instructions:

1. Place cooked orzo in a bowl, drizzle with olive oil. Stir. Add feta, olives, tomatoes, nuts and parsley on top. Toss these Ingredients together.

Add salt and pepper according to taste.

2. Chill for an hour and serve with choice of grilled veggies.

57. **Argula Salad**

Total Time: 15 minutes

Ingredients:

- 5.5 oz arugula
- 1 apple
- 5 walnuts
- 3.5 cheddar
- 1 tbsp mustard
- 2 tbsp olive oil
- 2 tbsp vinegar wine
- A pinch of pepper and salt

Instructions:

1.Wash apple and arugula, and peel the nuts. Chop apple into thin slices, and
cubed cheddar.
2.Prepare a salad dressing. Mix olive oil, vinegar, and mustard in a small bowl.
3.In a deep bowl, place arugula, apple, cheddar and nuts. Season with salt,
pepper, and salad dressing.

Nutrients per one serving:

Calories: 198 | Fats: 9 g | Carbs: 4.9 g | Proteins: 15 g

58.   **Beef and Lentil Chili**

Total Time: 1hr 10 min| Serves 4

Ingredients

- Ground beef – 2 pounds
- Chopped onion – 1
- Chopped stewed potatoes – 2 cans
- Minced cloves garlic – 1
- Chili powder – 3 tablespoons
- Dried and rinsed lentils – 1 cup
- Chili powder – 3 tablespoons

- Chocolate semisweet – 1 ounce
- Tomato sauce – 1 can
- Salt – ¼ teaspoon
- Water – 2 cups

Instructions

1. Use a Dutch oven to cook ground beef and onion over medium heat for 8 minutes or until the meat is pink.

2. Add garlic and then cook for a minute. After that, add the remaining ingredients apart from water and lentils and then cook and bring to a boil.

3. Add lentils and water. Reduce heat and allow to simmer for one hour as you stir often.

4. Serve with a dollop of sour cream, grated cheese or fresh onions.

Nutrients per one serving:

Calories per serving: 367; Carbohydrates: 29g; Protein: 29g; Fat: 16g; Sugar: 4g; Sodium: 655mg; Fiber: 6g

59. **Caprese**

Total Time: 15 minutes

Ingredients:

- 3 tomatoes
- 1.5 oz mozzarella
- 4.5 oz fresh spinach
- 2 tbsp olive oil
- 2 tsp balsamic vinegar
- A couple branches of fresh oregano
- A pinch of ground coriander and salt

Instructions:

1. Wash tomatoes and oregano. Cut tomatoes into quarters.
2. Tear spinach into small pieces, dice mozzarella.
3. In a separate container, mix oil, vinegar, spices, salt and ground oregano.
4. Put tomatoes, mozzarella, and spinach on a plate. Season with salad dressing and stir well.

Nutrients per one serving:

Calories: 154 | Fats: 11 g | Carbs: 4.3 g | Proteins: 17 g

60. Watermelon Salad

Total Time: 15 minutes

Ingredients:

- 12.5 watermelon pulp
- 10.5 cherry tomatoes
- 1 cucumber
- 7 oz feta
- A couple mint leaves
- 2 tbsp olive oil
- 1 tbsp balsamic vinegar
- A pinch of salt and spices

Instructions:

1.Wash and dry tomatoes and cucumber. Dice vegetables. Remove the seeds.

Dice the watermelon pulp. Place all Ingredients in a salad bowl.

2.Add the minced feta and mint leaves.

3.Season with oil, vinegar, salt, and spices. Stir and let it brew for 3 minutes.

Nutrients per one serving:

Calories: 257 | Fats: 10 g | Carbs: 7.9 g | Proteins: 18 g

61.   Mediterranean Chicken

Total Time: 25 min

Ingredients

- Boneless chicken breast halves – 4 6 ounces
- Pepper and salt – ¼ teaspoon
- Olive oil – 3 tablespoons

- Grape tomatoes – 1 pint
- Ripe olives – 16
- Capers drained – 3 tablespoons

Instructions

1.   Sprinkle chicken with salt and pepper. Place a skillet over medium heat and cook the chicken for 3 minutes on each side or until golden brown.

2.   Add olives, tomatoes and capers. Set the oven to 4750F and then bake for 15 minutes or until the thermometer reads 1700.

3.   Remove from the oven once ready and then serve and enjoy.

Nutrients per one serving:

Calories per serving: 336; Carbohydrates: 6g; Protein: 36g; Fat: 3g; Sugar: 4g; Sodium: 631mg; Fiber: 2g

62.   Carrot Mintmellow Salad

Total Time: 1 hour and 5 minutes

Ingredients:

- 1 cup coarsely grated carrots
- 1 tbsp olive oil
- 1 tbsp fresh lemon juice
- 1 tbsp chopped fresh mint
- 1 clove garlic, crushed
- Pinch of salt

Instructions:

1. In a bowl, toss all the Ingredients to coat. Chill for an hour. Serve.

63.   Spaghetti with Seafood

Total Time: 20 minutes

Ingredients:

- 7 oz spaghetti
- 7 oz seafood cocktail
- 5 cherry tomatoes
- 2 tbsp olive oil
- 2 tbsp dry white wine
- 1 garlic clove
- A couple of basil twigs
- A pinch of black ground pepper and salt

Instructions:

1.Boil water for cooking spaghetti.

2.Wash cherry tomatoes, cut in half and fry for 3 minutes with chopped garlic.

3.Boil the spaghetti slightly until cooked for 5 minutes.

4.Drench seafood cocktail with boiled water and add to tomatoes. Stew for 3

minutes.

5.Merge spaghetti in a colander and place to the dressing. Stir well. Season

with wine and basil. Stew for 3 minutes. **Nutrients per one serving:** Calories: 238 | Fats: 17 g | Carbs: 6.2 g | Proteins: 20 g

64.   **Greek Style Ravioli**

Total Time: 25 min

Ingredients

- Frozen cheese ravioli – 12
- Lean ground beef – 1/3 pound
- Fresh baby spinach – 1 cup
- Sliced ripe olives – ¼ cup
- Crumbled feta cheese – ¼ cup
- Canned diced tomatoes with oregano, basil and garlic – 1 cup

Instructions

1.   Cook ravioli according to the Instructions given in the package and then drain. Place a skillet over medium heat. Cook beef for 6 minutes or until no longer pink.

2.   Stir in tomatoes. Bring to a boil. Reduce heat and then allow to simmer uncovered for 10 minutes as you occasionally stir.

3.   Add spinach, ravioli and olives. After which, heat through as you stir gently to combine. Sprinkle with cheese once ready.

4.   Serve and enjoy.

Nutrients per one serving:

Calories per serving: 333; Carbohydrates: 28g; Protein: 23g; Fat: 12g; Sugar: 4g; Sodium:851mg; Fiber: 2g

65.   Black Bean and Mango Salad

TOTAL TIME: 25 minutes

Ingredients:

- ½   cup canned black beans, rinsed and drained ¼ cup diced fresh mango

- ¼ cup cooked lentils
- ¼ cup diced red bell pepper
- ½   cup seeded, minced jalapeno pepper
- 2 tbsp minced red onion
- 1 tbsp lime juice
- 1 tbsp minced fresh cilantro
- 1 tbsp orange juice
- tbsp garlic-infused extra virgin olive oil Pinch of salt

Instructions:

1.   In a serving bowl, add the Ingredients listed and combine well.

2.   Chill for about 20 minutes. Serve.

Nutrients per one serving:

180 Calories, 7g fat, 290mg sodium, 25g carbohydrate, 7g protein.

66.   Cucumber-Salmon Salad

TOTAL TIME: 5 minutes

Ingredients:

- 1 large cucumber
- 3 thinly sliced radishes
- 2 thinly sliced smoked salmon
- 3 tbsp Italian dressing
- 3 tbsp olives, pitted
- 2 tbsp chopped red onions
- ¼ cup crumbled feta cheese with basil and tomato

Instructions:

1. Using a vegetable peeler, cut cucumber into long thin ribbons. Place in a bowl and add all the remaining ingredients. Toss and drape smoke salmon to the top and serve as desired.

67. Taltali Baked Rice

TOTAL TIME: 40 minutes

Ingredients:

- 1 cup cooked medium-grain brown rice ¼ cup cubed artichoke hearts
- ¼ cup asparagus pieces, blanched 2 tbsp diced roasted red pepper ¼ cup sun-dried tomatoes in oil 2 tbsp diced goat cheese
- 2 tsp red wine vinegar
- 1 tbsp extra virgin olive oil
- 2 tsp fresh minced parsley
- Salt and pepper to taste

Instructions:

1.   Preheat oven to 375 degrees F.

2.   In a bowl, combine rice, artichokes, tomatoes, asparagus, goat cheese and pepper. Mix. Add olive oil, red wine vinegar, parsley, salt and pepper. Toss to combine.

3.   Spread the mixture into a casserole dish. Bake for 25-30 minutes until cheese begins to brown lightly.

4.   Serve warm.

68. Rice and Shrimps

Total Time: 15 minutes

Ingredients:

- 2 cups white rice
- 7 oz boiled shrimps
- 2 tbsp olive oil
- 2 eggs
- 1 cup frozen peas
- 1 green onion
- 2 garlic cloves
- 2 tbsp rice vinegar
- 3 tbsp soy sauce
- 1 tsp ground ginger
- ½ tsp ground allspice
- A pinch of salt

Instructions:

1. Heat deep frying pan; add 1 tbsp oil. Season shrimps with salt and pepper.
Fry for 3 minutes. Place on a plate.

2. Add oil and fry chopped green onion, garlic and ginger powder. Fry for 2
minutes.

3. Add washed rice into the frying pan, stir and simmer for 2 minutes.

4.Add the eggs, stir and fry for another 2 minutes. Add peas, vinegar, soy

sauce, ½ cup of water and simmer until rice is ready. Add shrimps and steam again for 3 minutes. Sprinkle rice with green onion.

Nutrients per one serving:

Calories: 298 | Fats: 18 g | Carbs: 7.5 g | Proteins: 22 g

69.　Baked Cod and Olives

Total Time: 25 minutes

Ingredients:

- 1 lb cod fillet
- 5 cherry tomatoes
- 3.5 oz pitted green olives
- 2 tbsp capers
- 2 fresh thyme branches
- 3 tbsp olive oil
- 2 tbsp balsamic vinegar
- A pinch of salt
- A pinch of pepper mix
- Salad leaves

Instructions:

1.Cut the fish fillet into portions. Grease a form and place the fish. Add toma-

toes, olives, capers, and thyme.

2.Season all Ingredients with oil, vinegar, spices, and salt.

3.Bake in the oven at 210°C 410°F for 15 minutes.

4.Remove from oven, cover with foil on top and back again for 3 minutes.

5.Place on a plate and decorate with salad leaves.

Nutrients per one serving:

Calories: 234 | Fats: 18 g | Carbs: 5.9 g | Proteins: 24 g

70. Herb Roasted Olives and Tomatoes

Total Time: 20 min

Ingredients

- Cherry tomatoes – 2 cups
- Garlic stuffed olives – 1 cup
- Greek olives – 1 cup
- Pitted ripe olives – 1 cup
- Peeled garlic cloves – 8
- Olive oil – 3 tablespoons
- Herbes de provence – 1 tablespoon
- Pepper – 1 teaspoon

Instructions

1.   Get the oven preheated to 4250 and then combine all the Ingredients apart from olive oil and seasonings into a greased baking pan.

2.   Add oil and seasonings to the mixture and then toss to coat. Roast the mixture for 20 minutes or until the tomatoes become soft as you occasionally stir.

3.   Serve and enjoy.

Nutrients per one serving:

Calories: 153; Carbohydrates: 9g; Protein: 8g; Fat: 6g; Sugar: 2g; Sodium:250mg; Fiber: 2g

71. Fennel Seafood Paella

TOTAL TIME: 40 minutes

Ingredients:

- ½ cup scallops, hard muscle removed
- ½ cup small shrimps, peeled and deveined
- ½ cup whole wheat couscous
- ¼ cup vegetable broth
- 1 cup diced tomatoes, unsalted, with juice

- 1 tbsp extra virgin olive oil
- 1 onion, chopped
- 1 clove garlic, minced
- Pinch of salt and pepper
- ½ tsp each dried thyme and fennel seeds Pinch of crumbled saffron threads

Instructions:

1.   Heat oil in a skillet on medium heat. Cook onion for about 2-3 minutes. Add minced garlic, fennel seeds, dried thyme, saffron, a pinch of salt and pepper. Sauté for about 20 seconds.

2.   Pour in vegetable broth and tomatoes. Simmer covered for 2 minutes in reduced heat.

3.   Increase heat to medium and add scallops. Cook for 2 minutes and add in shrimp, cook stirring for 2 minutes more. Stir in couscous, cover and remove from heat. Let it stand for about 5 minutes and fluff.

4. Serve.

Nutrients per one serving:

409 Calories, 7g total fat 1g sat, 4g mono , 103mg cholesterol, 584mg sodium, 59g carbohydrate, 10g dietary fiber, 399mg potassium.

72.   Moroccan Apple Beef Stew

Total Time: 2hrs 20 min| Serves 8

Ingredients

- Beef stew meat – 1 ½ pounds cut into pieces
- Ground allspice – ¼ teaspoon
- Ground cinnamon – ½ teaspoon
- Pepper and salt to taste
- Olive oil – 3 tablespoons
- Large onion – 1
- Minced garlic cloves – 3
- Beef broth – 1 can
- Pitted dried plums – 1 cup chopped
- Gala apples peeled – 2 cut into 1 ½ inch pieces
- Tomato sauce – 1 can
- Honey – 1 tablespoon
- Hot cooked rice or couscous optional

Instructions

1.   Mix together the cinnamon, salt, pepper and allspice and then use the mixture to toss and coat the beef.

2.	Place a Dutch oven over medium heat and then add 2 tablespoons of olive oil. After that, cook the beef until browned. Remove the beef from the pan using a slotted spoon.

3.	Add onions to the pan and cook for about 6 minutes or until tender and then add garlic and cook for a minute longer. Add tomato sauce, dried plums, broth and honey and cook for a minute.

4.	Return beef into the pan and then bring to boil for about one and a half hours on reduced heat as you let it simmer while covered.

5.	Add apples and then cook for about 45 minutes or until the apples and beef are tender.

6.	You can then serve the stew with rice or your preferred dish.

Nutrients per one serving:

Calories per serving: 339; Carbohydrates: 24g; Protein: 29g; Fat: 13g; Sugar: 8g; Sodium:905mg; Fiber: 2g

73. **Fried Tuna**

Total Time: 15 minutes

Ingredients:
- 2 tuna steaks
- 2 zucchini
- 1 eggplant
- 5 cherry tomatoes
- 1 garlic clove
- 2 tbsp olive oil
- 2 tbsp olives
- A pinch of salt and spices

Instructions:

1.Wash and cut vegetables into small cubes. Preheat a frying pan with olive oil.

Fry the eggplant and zucchini for 5 minutes.

2.Add chopped garlic, spices and salt. Stew for one minutes.

3.Fry a tuna for 5 minutes on both sides.

4.Place vegetables and fried tuna on ta plate. Add chopped olives and halves

of tomatoes.

Nutrients per one serving: Calories: 269 | Fats: 21 g | Carbs: 6 g | Proteins: 25 g

74. **Chicken and Broccoli**

Total Time: 35 minutes

Ingredients:

- 2 lbs chicken breast
- 1 broccoli head
- 1 bell pepper
- 2 tbsp peanut butter
- 5 oz olive oil
- 2 tbsp soy sauce
- 2 tbsp rice vinegar
- 2 tbsp liquid honey
- 1 tbsp lime juice
- 1 tsp sesame
- 3.5 oz green onion
- A pinch of salt

Instructions:

1.Preheat the oven to 210°C 410°F . Cover a baking sheet with parchment.

2.Wash and dry up chicken. Beat with a hammer, season with salt and place
on a baking sheet.

3.Divide broccoli into inflorescences, season with salt and oil. Place near the

chicken meat. Peel peppers from the seeds and chop into

thin slices. Grease and place near the broccoli.

4.Bake chicken breast with vegetables for 25 minutes.

5.In the bowl, mix peanut butter, soy sauce, vinegar, honey, lemon juice and 3

tablespoons of water. Heat sauce slowly.

6.Season chicken breast with hot sauce, decorate with

sesame and chopped onion.

Nutrients per one serving:

Calories: 254 | Fats: 18 g | Carbs: 4 g | Proteins: 21 g

75. Turkey with Mushrooms

Total Time: 35 minutes

Ingredients:

- 1 lb turkey fillet
- 2 onions
- 10.5 oz Portobello
- 2 tbsp butter
- 1 cup cream
- A pinch of ground allspice

- A pinch of salt

Instructions:

1.Peel and cut mushrooms into quarters. Peel and chop the onion into half

rings. Cube turkey fillet.

2.Fry meat in a frying pan with butter for 4 minutes. Stir well. Add salt and

pepper.

3.Transfer fillet on a plate. Fry onion with mushrooms in high heat for 7 min-

utes. Season with salt and pepper.

4.Add fillet and cream to mushroom sauce, and stir well. Stew on low heat for

10 minutes.

Nutrients per one serving: Calories: 257 | Fats: 17 g | Carbs: 6.5 g | Proteins: 26 g

76.   **Baked Eggplants**

Total Time: 40 minutes

Ingredients:

- 3 eggplants
- 3 tbsp olive oil
- 3 garlic cloves
- 1 tsp ground paprika
- A bunch of rosemary
- A pinch of salt
- 3 tbsp sour cream

Instructions:

1.Wash eggplants and not peel. Cut them lengthways in half. Season with salt and leave for 7 minutes.

2.Grind rosemary and garlic and add oil.

3.Put the eggplants on the baking sheet and make small cuts with a knife. Sea-

son with oil and rosemary. Bake for 25 minutes at 200°C 392°F .

4.In a deep bowl, mix sour cream, sweet pepper, and salt. Season eggplants

with sour cream sauce.

Nutrients per one serving: Calories: 168 | Fats: 12 g | Carbs: 3.2 g | Proteins: 15 g

77.   **Mediterranean Chickpeas**

Total Time: 25 min| Serves 4

Ingredients

- Whole wheat couscous – ¾ cup
- Chopped medium onion – 1
- Olive oil – 1 tablespoon
- Minced cloves garlic – 2
- Chickpeas – 1 can rinsed and drained
- Stewed tomatoes – 1 can
- Water packed artichoke hearts chopped, rinsed and drained – 1 can
- Pitted Greek olives coarsely chopped – ½ cup
- Dried oregano – ½ teaspoon
- Dash of pepper and cayenne

- Lemon juice – 1 tablespoon
- Water – 1 cup

Instructions

1.   Place a saucepan over medium heat and then add water and bring to a boil. Add couscous to the boiling water. Allow to stay for 2 minutes and then remove from heat.

2.   Let the couscous stay in the saucepan and absorb all the water for about 10 minutes. It should be easy to fluff with a fork.

3.   Place a skillet over medium heat and then add olive oil. Add onion and then cook until tender. Add garlic and cook for one more minute.

4.   Stir in the remaining ingredients and then let it heat through as you stir occasionally.

5.   Serve with couscous and enjoy.

Nutrients per one serving:

Calories per serving: 340; Carbohydrates: 41g; Protein: 11g; Fat: 10g; Sugar: 8g; Sodium:677mg; Fiber: 7g

78. Quinoa Tabbouleh

Total Time: 35 min| Serves 8
Ingredients

- Quinoa rinsed – 1 cup
- Black beans rinsed and drained – 1 can
- Water – 2 cups
- Cucumber peeled and chopped – 1 small
- Freshly minced parsley – 1/3 cup
- Olive oil – 2 tablespoons
- Lemon juice ¼ cup
- Sweet red pepper chopped – 1
- Salt and pepper – ½ teaspoon

Instructions

1.   Bring water to a boil in a large saucepan and then add quinoa. Reduce the heat. Allow to simmer covered for 15 minutes or until liquid is absorbed.

2.   Remove from the heat and then fluff with a fork and transfer into a bowl in order to cool.

3.   Add cucumber, beans, parsley and red pepper. After that, in a small bowl, mix together the remaining ingredients and then drizzle over the salad and toss to coat.

4.   Refrigerate until chilled. You can then enjoy it as desired.

Nutrients per one serving:

Calories 159; Carbohydrates: 24g; Protein: 6g; Fat: 5g; Sugar: 8g; Sodium:255mg; Fiber: 4g

79. Mediterranean Quesadillas

Total Time: 20 min| Serves 2

Ingredients

- Tortillas – 2 8 inch
- Shredded mozzarella – 1 cup
- Crumbled feta – ¼ cup
- Baby spinach – ¼ cup
- Artichoke hearts sliced – ¼ cup
- Sundried tomatoes thinly sliced – 2 tablespoons
- Sliced kalamata olives – 2 tablespoons
- Romesco sauce – 1 tablespoon optional

Instructions

1.   Place a pan over medium heat and then add a tortilla into the pan. Sprinkle half of cheese and then follow with spinach, feta, artichoke hearts, kalamata olives, sundried tomatoes, the remaining cheese and the remaining tortilla.

2.   Cook for about 4 minutes or until the quesadilla is golden brown on both sides and the cheese melted.

3.   Serve and enjoy.

Nutrients per one serving:

Calories per serving: 304; Carbohydrates: 33g; Protein: 25g; Fat: 8g; Sugar: 4g; Sodium:840mg; Fiber: 4g

80. Spanish Garlic Shrimp

Total Time: 20 min| Serves 4

Ingredients

- Olive oil – 1/3 cup
- Large shrimp peeled and deveined – 1 pound
- Sweet Spanish paprika – 1 teaspoon
- Chili flakes – ¼ teaspoon
- Kosher salt – ¼ teaspoon
- Finely chopped cloves garlic – 4
- Dry sherry – 2 tablespoons
- Fresh lemon juice – 1 ½ tablespoons
- Chopped parsley – 2 tablespoons

Instructions

1.   Place a skillet over medium heat and then pour in olive oil and heat. Add garlic and chili flakes. After that, cook for a minute over high heat.

2.   Once garlic is fragrant, add shrimp into the pan and then season with salt, pepper and paprika.

3.   Cook the shrimp as you stir often for about 5 minutes or until it turns pink. Add lemon juice and sherry. Cook for 3 more minutes or until liquid is reduced and shrimp well cooked.

4.   Sprinkle parsley on top and then serve with some crusty bread or your preferred dish.

Nutrients per one serving:

Calories 250; Carbohydrates: 3g; Protein: 16g; Fat: 17g; Sugar: 4g; Sodium:840mg; Fiber: 4g

81. Mediterranean Spiced Salmon and Vegetable Quinoa

Total Time: 30 min

Ingredients

For Quinoa

- Quinoa – 1 cup
- Sliced cherry tomatoes – 1 cup
- Finely dried red onion – ¼ cup
- Kosher salt – ½ teaspoon
- Thinly sliced basil leaves – 4
- Lemon zest -1
- Diced and seeded cucumbers – ¾ cup

Salmon

- Salmon fillets – 20 ounces
- Chopped fresh parsley – ¼ cup
- Paprika – ½ teaspoon
- Cumin – 1 teaspoon
- Salmon fillets – 20 ounces
- Lemon wedges – 8
- Salt and pepper – ¼ teaspoon

Instructions

1.   Place a saucepan over medium heat and then add 2 cups water, quinoa and salt. Bring to a boil.

2.   Cover the saucepan and then reduce the heat to simmer for 20 minutes.

3.   Turn the heat off and allow it to stay for 5 minutes while still covered before serving.

4. Before serving, mix the tomatoes, cucumbers, basil, onions and lemon zest.

5. In a different bowl, combine salt and pepper, cumin and paprika. Next, line a pan with foil and grease lightly with olive oil.

6. Transfer salmon fillets into the pan. Coat evenly the fillet with the spice mixture.

7. Place salmon wedges on the edge of the pan alongside salmon and then broil on high for about 10 minutes with the rack placed at the lower third of the oven.

8. Remove once time is up or when salmon is well cooked and flakes apart with a fork.

9. Sprinkle it with parsley. Serve with the roasted lemon wedges and the prepared vegetable quinoa.

Nutrients per one serving:

Calories 222; Carbohydrates: 16g; Protein: 32g; Fat: 4g; Sugar: 2g; Sodium:753mg; Fiber: 2g

82.   Easy Mediterranean Chicken

Total Time 30 min|Serves 4

Ingredients

- Large boneless and skinless chicken – 2lbs
- Dried oregano – 1 tablespoon
- Smoked paprika – 1 teaspoon
- Himalayan salt – 1 teaspoon
- Freshly ground black pepper – 1 teaspoon
- Mini bell peppers of different colors – 6
- Diced medium tomatoes – 2
- Seeded and sliced jalapeno peppers - 2
- Sliced green onions – 2 tablespoons
- Lime juice

Instructions:

1.   Get the oven preheated to 4500F.

2.   Have all the mixed in a small bowl and then marinate the chicken thighs with the spice mix.

3.   In a baking dish, place the chicken and add vegetables on the side.

4.   Cover the baking dish with aluminum foil. Bake for about 35 minutes.

5.　　Set the oven to broil and then remove the foil and cook again for another 5 minutes or until the chicken becomes golden.

6.　　Slice the chicken. Serve as you top with vegetables.

Nutrients per one serving:

Calories 293; Carbohydrates: 6g; Protein: 20g; Fat: 15g; Sugar: 0g; Sodium: 201mg; Fiber: 0g

83.   Salmon with Broccoli and Lemon Mayo

Total Time: 25 min

Ingredients

- Salmon – 1 ½ lbs
- Broccoli – 1 lb
- Butter – 2 oz
- Salt and water
- Mayonnaise – 1 cup
- Lemon juice – 2 tablespoons

Instructions

1.   Mix lemon juice and mayonnaise. Set aside for later use.

2.   Divide salmon into pieces. Season with salt and pepper.

3.   Over medium heat, fry salmon with half of the butter for about 10 minutes on both sides and then lower the heat towards the end. Remove salmon from the pan and keep warm.

4.   Trim and rinse broccoli, including the stem and then have them chopped into bite-sized pieces.

5.   Add the remaining butter in the used skillet and then cook broccoli for 4 minutes over medium heat or until softened slightly and golden brown.

6.   Season the broccoli with salt and pepper.

7.   Serve the salmon with broccoli and a dollop of mayo.

Nutrients per one serving:

Calories: 560; Carbohydrates: 3g; Protein: 29g; Fat: 68g; Sugar: 0g; Sodium:540mg; Fiber: 2g

84. Easy Orange Harissa Lamb Chops

Total Time: 30 min| Serves 6

Ingredients

- Frenched lamb rack – 2.25lm
- Extra virgin olive oil –
- Orange slices for garnish
- Fresh parsley for garnish
- For Spice Mixture
- Harissa spice blend – 2 teaspoons
- Black pepper – 1 teaspoon
- Salt – ½ teaspoon
- Ground coriander -1/2 teaspoon

- Ground cinnamon – ½ teaspoon
- For Marinade
- Zested and juiced orange – 1
- Zested and juiced lemon – 1
- Virgin oil – ¼ cup
- Minced garlic cloves – 10
- Tahini sauce for serving optional

Instructions

1.   In a bowl, combine harissa spice blend, coriander, salt, pepper and cinnamon and then make a spice mixture.

2.   Use the spice mixture to rub on the lamb chops on both sides and then place the lamb chops into a zip lock bag.

3.   Mix the Ingredients for marinade together. Add it into the zip lock bag with the lamb chops. Add the remaining spices into the zip lock as well.

4.   Zip the bag and then use your hands to coat the lamb chops well. Leave it at room temperature for about 20 minutes.

5.   Place a large skillet over medium heat. Add olive oil and heat to shimmering. Add lamb chops to the skillet and then sear for 3 minutes on each side, depending on the thickness of the lamb chops. You can still cook longer as desired.

6.   Transfer the lamb chops to a platter and then cover with foil. Repeat the process with the remaining chops until all are done.

7.   Garnish with fresh parsley leaves and thinly sliced oranges. Add a drizzle of tahini sauce if desired and enjoy.

Nutrients per one serving:

Calories: 132; Carbohydrates: 4g; Protein: 13g; Fat: 8g; Sugar: 2g; Sodium:204mg; Fiber: 1g

85.   Greek Lamb Chops

Total Time 18 Mins

Ingredients

- 1/2 teaspoon salt
- 1/2 teaspoon ground cumin
- 1/4 teaspoon ground coriander
- 1/4 teaspoon black pepper
- 1/8 teaspoon ground cinnamon
- 8 (4-ounce) lamb loin chops, trimmed Cooking spray
- 2 tablespoons finely chopped pistachios
- 2 tablespoons chopped fresh flat-leaf parsley
- 1 tablespoon chopped fresh cilantro

- 2 teaspoons grated lemon rind
- 1/8 teaspoon salt 1 garlic clove, minced

Instructions:

1 Heat a large nonstick skillet over medium-high heat. Combine first 5 ingredients; sprinkle evenly over both sides of lamb. Coat pan with cooking spray. Add lamb to pan; cook 4 minutes on each side or until desired degree of doneness.

2 While lamb cooks, combine pistachios and the remaining ingredients; sprinkle over lamb.

Nutrients per one serving:

Calories 233 Fat 11.2g Satfat 3.5g Monofat 5g Polyfat 1.2g Protein 29.6g Carbohydrate 1.9g Fiber 0.8g Cholesterol 90mg Iron 2.4mg Sodium 467mg Calcium 32mg

86.   Easy Cucumber Soup

Total Time 15 minutes

Ingredients

- 1 3/4 lbs cucumber peeled, seeded and cut into 3" pieces
- 1/4 red onion roughly chopped
- 1 clove garlic skinned
- 8 large mint leaves
- 1 tsp maple syrup
- 2 Tbl lemon juice
- 3/4 cup unsweetened homemade yogurt (or a small container store-bought)
- 1/2 cup water or more
- 1 avocado chopped
- sea salt to taste

Instructions:

Place all the ingredients except the avocado in a Vitamix or food processor with 1/2 cup of the spring water. Pulse a few times so the INGREDIENTS are coarsely chopped, then process until smooth. Thin with more water if needed.

Transfer to a bowl an refrigerate 2 hours or overnight, until well chilled.

Ladle soup into soup bowls and top with the chopped avocado.

Nutrients per one serving:

Calories 68 Calories from Fat 9 , Total Fat 1g 2% Carbohydrates 13.9g 5% Protein 2.6g 5% Vitamin 25% ,Calcium 9%

87. Saffron Fish Stew With White Beans

Total Time 20 Mins

Ingredients

- 1 tablespoon extra-virgin olive oil
- 1 cup prechopped onion
- 1 teaspoon ground fennel
- 1/2 teaspoon ground coriander
- 2 garlic cloves, crushed 1 thyme sprig
- 1/2 teaspoon grated fresh orange rind
- 1/4 teaspoon saffron threads, crushed

- 1 1/2 cups water
- 1 1/2 cups clam juice
- 1 (14.5-ounce) can diced tomatoes, undrained
- 1/8 teaspoon salt
- 1 pound flounder fillet, cut into (2-inch) pieces
- 1 (14-ounce) can great Northern beans, rinsed and drained Fresh thyme leaves

Instructions:

Heat oil in a large Dutch oven over medium-high heat. Add onion, fennel, coriander, garlic, and thyme sprig; sauté 5 minutes. Stir in rind and saffron; add water, clam juice, and tomatoes. Bring to a boil; reduce heat, and simmer for 5 minutes. Stir in salt, fish, and beans; cook 5 minutes. Top with thyme leaves.

Nutrients per one serving:

Calories 249 Fat 5.1g Satfat 0.9g Monofat 2.8g Polyfat 0.9g Protein 27.9g Carbohydrate 23g Fiber 5.7g Cholesterol 57mg Iron 2.2mg Sodium 495mg Calcium 101mg

Lightning Source UK Ltd.
Milton Keynes UK
UKHW020630280521
384530UK00001B/188